TALES OF ST. PATRICK

TALES OF ST. PATRICK

❧

EILEEN DUNLOP

Holiday House / New York

Library of Congress Cataloging-in-Publication Data
Dunlop, Eileen.
Tales of St. Patrick / by Eileen Dunlop.
p.   cm.
Summary: A fictionalized account of the life of Saint Patrick,
first Bishop of Ireland, from the time he was taken to Ireland as a
slave when he was sixteen years old through his life-long efforts to
Christianize the Irish people.
ISBN 0-8234-1218-0 (hc : alk. paper)
1. Patrick, Saint, 373?–463?—Juvenile fiction.   [1. Patrick,
Saint, 373?–463?—Fiction.   2. Ireland—History—To 1172—Fiction.]
I. Title.
PZ7.D9214Tal   1996   95-35087   CIP   AC
[Fic]—dc20

For Lucille Rose

Author's Note

Although Patrick is among the most famous people who ever lived, not much is known about him for certain. Modern scholars have agreed that he lived and worked in Ireland in the fifth century, but have disagreed about the dates of his birth and death, his birthplace, his education and the extent of his travels. Some facts about Patrick's life can be found in his own *Confession*, but many of the best-known stories about him are clearly legends. The nature of the boyhood sin which caused him so much trouble in later years is unknown.

I have written this book on the assumption that Patrick was active in the years when the Romans were withdrawing from northern Europe, leaving behind them chaos from which Ireland was happily exempt. As well as Patrick's own writings I have used other ancient sources, chiefly the seventh-century Lives written by Tíreachán and Muirchú. The names of Patrick's "household" come from a list in the *Annals of the Four Masters*.

In Patrick's time, many places had names different from those they have today. Here are some of the places mentioned in this book and their modern counterparts.

Roman (Latin)

Monavia	Isle of Man
Sabrina	Severn
Deva	Chester
Eburacum	York
Aralensis	Isle of Lérins
Autissiodorum	Auxerre
Caledonia	Scotland
Gaul (Gallia)	France

Irish

Ard Mhacha	Armagh
Sabhall	Saul
Dún Leathghlaise	Downpatrick

Contents

TALES OF ST. PATRICK

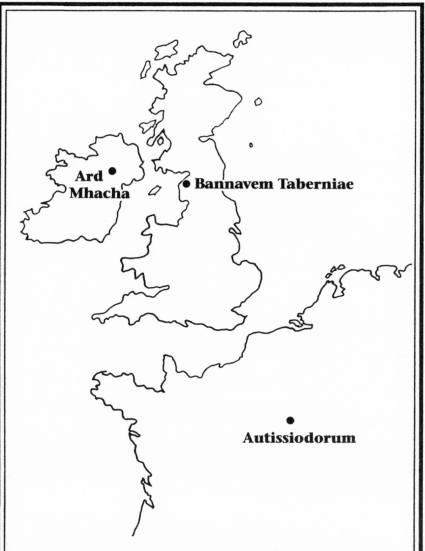

Patrick's birthplace, which he called *Bannavem Taberniae*, was probably on the west coast of the country now known as Britain.

Autissiodorum in Gaul (France) where he was educated, is now called Auxerre.

Ard Mhacha, where Patrick made his headquarters on the hill of Droim Sailech, is now the cathedral city of Armagh, in the north of Ireland.

1

Sucat

⊗

One day at sea, and already it seemed eternity. Huddled under a filthy blanket, listening to the fearsome creaking of the ship and the groans of his fellow captives, Sucat could scarcely believe that only yesterday he hadn't had a care in the world. Sometimes he had thought that today was a bad dream from which he would wake up. Most of the time he had known that it wasn't.

Yesterday. It had been a perfect spring day, with soft green shoots among the winter grass and a breeze tossing clouds and seagulls across the pale blue sky. There had even been some warmth in the midday sun. Sucat and his friend Dion had enjoyed their fishing expedition among the hills, but afternoon had brought a sudden chill. Summer was still some way off.

"Let's go home now," Sucat had said, shivering in his sleeveless tunic. Dion had agreed. While he divided the trout they had caught and strung them on two pieces of line, Sucat collected the tackle and the remains of their picnic lunch. "That was fun," he said,

1

pulling on his warm woollen cloak. "We'll come again tomorrow if the weather stays fine."

Dion nodded and the two boys began to scramble upstream towards the crest of the hill. At the top they paused to get their breath back and admire the view. Away to the north they could make out the dark, undulating line of the great Roman wall. To the south, tucked snugly into a fold of hillside, lay Sucat's father's villa and the farm-village of Bannavem Taberniae where Dion lived. Westward the sea was pink and pewter under the sinking sun, its misty horizon bisected by the inky mass of the island of Monavia. There were sails far out, but there was so much coming and going between the island and the mainland that neither Sucat nor Dion paid them any attention. Whistling and swinging the fish, they dropped down through the withered bracken towards home.

"See you tomorrow, then?" said Dion, as they reached the entrance to the villa.

There was a hopeful note in his voice, and Sucat knew that he wanted to be invited in. The warm baths, comfortable couches and good dinners of Councillor Calpornius's house were treats for the farm labourer's son who had no luxuries at home. But Sucat, although he liked Dion, only gave him treats when he was in the mood. Now he was tired, and wanted the rest of the day to himself.

So he said, "Right. Usual time," and pushed open the heavy wooden gate.

Afterwards he would often wish that he had been kinder, and said goodbye less abruptly. But he couldn't possibly have known, as he latched the gate behind

2

him, that he and Dion would never see each other
again.

The Irish raiders had come at dawn. Shipping their oars
and dropping anchor in the shallows beneath the cliff,
they swarmed silently ashore in the thin grey light. At
the hour when sleep was deepest and their victims
least prepared, they drew their swords and fell upon
the village. Blood-freezing cries mingled with the
screams and prayers of people whose worst nightmare
had come true. Sucat, who had gone to bed late after a
heavy supper, was woken by shouts of alarm in the
courtyard of the villa, and the acrid smell of smoke as
the attackers torched the roof. Leaping naked out of
bed, he pulled on his tunic and ran into the hall. To
his dismay he saw two burly, red-bearded pirates
dragging his sister Lupita towards the door. Lupita was
weeping and calling shrilly for help.

"Father, save me! Mother! Sucat!"

"Leave her alone," yelled Sucat furiously, launching
himself with clenched fists across the tiled floor.

He might as well have saved his breath. He too was
roughly seized and manhandled through the smoke-
filled courtyard into the road. There dozens – though it
seemed to the horrified Sucat like thousands – of
frightened men, women and children were being
herded at sword-point towards the shore. Sucat looked
in vain for his parents, and lost sight of Lupita as he
stumbled down the cliff path. Cries of pain and terror
seemed to sear his brain. He was pushed across the
shingle and felt water lapping icily around his bare
legs. Then he was tumbled, with ten or so others, over

the side and into the bottom of a curach.

Trembling with cold and dazed with misfortune, Sucat scrambled up from his knees as the flamboyant Irishmen, gleeful at the success of their raid, pushed the vessel out and sprang aboard. Helped by the prevailing wind they raised the brown sail, and soon the curach was cutting through the waves towards the distant coast of Ireland.

Through a mist of tears, Sucat looked back at the hills of home and the sinister column of black smoke swaying above the ruins of Bannavem Taberniae. Not knowing what had happened to his parents and Lupita was terrible, but he was also overwhelmed by pity for himself. All his life Sucat had been pampered, a rich boy with nothing more important on his mind than having a good time. Today he had expected to go fishing with Dion, returning as usual to a hot bath and a good evening meal. Instead he was a prisoner on board a pirate ship, bound for a life of slavery in an unknown land.

2

The Wood of Foclath

⊗

Just as he found it hard to remember how long he had been at sea, Sucat soon lost track of the days he had spent working for the Irish chieftain Míleac mac Boin. Míleac, a gruff, long-haired man in a checked tunic and sheepskin cloak, had bought him from the raiders who had captured him. Sucat would never forget the humiliation of standing tethered like an animal at market while farmers looked him over, sneering at his thin body and smooth white hands. Sucat had found their language difficult to understand, but their opinion was clear enough.

"Did you ever see such a weakling? Just look at his skinny legs!"

"And his knock-knees! You wouldn't get much work out of that one."

"You're right. Too soft to get his hands dirty, if you ask me."

Míleac had seemed to think differently. He paid for Sucat, put him in a cart and transported him over miles of rough green countryside. At last they arrived at Míleac's fortified farmstead beside the Wood of Foclath. Sucat could hear the familiar sound of the sea, but he had no idea which sea, or how far he was from home.

Míleac knew enough Latin to communicate with his new slave.

"What's your name?"

Bravado hadn't entirely forsaken Sucat.

"Patricius," he announced, lifting his chin haughtily.

Although he had always been called "Sucat" by his family and friends, he was proud of his Roman name which meant "noble". The funny side of this wasn't lost on Míleac, who raised his thick eyebrows and grinned.

"Noble? Not here you're not," he retorted, but then added, "Let it be 'Patrick', then. Well, Patrick, your job will be to look after my sheep. Guard them well and see that none are carried off by wolves, or it will be the worse for you."

"Yes, sir," replied Patrick, tight-lipped.

Though he was pleased with his new name, calling a man like Míleac "Sir" stuck in his throat. He tried not to shudder visibly at the mention of wolves. He felt far more afraid for himself than for Míleac's sheep.

For a while Patrick was in the depths of despair, sullen and resentful at the unfairness of what had happened to him. Instead of having slaves to look after him he was now a slave himself, the property of a man he secretly despised as uncouth. After sixteen years of luxury he had to get used to living in a hut with a leaking roof and spaces in the wattle walls where the wind whistled through. His food, carried up to him in a basket by a kitchen slave, was barley cake, rancid meat and an occasional lump of cheese. It was a dramatic change for a Roman citizen, used to a privileged life in the years before the legions withdrew to defend the besieged city of Rome.

As the days went by, however, a change gradually came over Patrick. Perhaps having a different name helped him to live in the present and stop grieving for the past. Also, for the first time in his life he experienced quiet. Instead of going to school in town, larking about with other boys and enjoying rowdy games more than lessons, out in the pasture with his sheep he had time to think. Although his family was Christian – his father was a deacon and his grandfather had been a priest – Patrick had always been bored by religion. He had skipped family prayers and paid little attention to the Scriptures.

Now, as he sat at the door of his hut on starlit nights, listening to the wind in the trees and the invisible sea crashing on to the shore, words that his mother had long ago read to him from the Psalms returned to him. It was God, he remembered, who stretched out the heavens like a curtain, who walked upon the wings of the wind and covered the earth with a garment of sea.

As he counted his sheep in the evening, helping the lambs over the wall into the safety of the fold, he remembered that God had been described as a good shepherd. When he was homesick and wolves howled eerily in the wood, he comforted himself with the words, *I will say of the Lord, he is my refuge and my fortress; my God, in him will I trust.* Patrick began to hear God's voice in the wind and the waves, and he began to confide in God.

The days of Patrick's first summer in Ireland shortened and autumn painted the Wood of Foclath crimson and gold. One night Patrick had a strange dream. He had confessed to God how bad he now felt about the wasted opportunities of the past, how he wished he had studied harder and played the fool less. God hadn't seemed to answer and Patrick was feeling guilty and depressed. Then he dreamt that he was imprisoned under a huge stone, lying in a deep, muddy hole. This was frightening, but before Patrick had time to panic strong hands reached down and lifted the stone. There was a wall nearby and the hands, which Patrick knew were God's, carried the stone over and set it firmly on top. When he woke, Patrick realised that God had sent him a message through the dream.

"You are like a stone," God said, "which tumbled off my wall and lay for a long time in the mud. Now I have lifted you up and put you back in a high place. I have forgiven your past foolishness, and in the future I shall give you important work to do."

The vain Sucat of Bannavem Taberniae would have been cock-a-hoop, thinking how wise God was to recognise him as a future leader of men. The slave Patrick saw things differently. He had the sense to realise that whatever the future might bring, his duty now was to serve Míleac, his earthly master. So he concentrated on being a good shepherd, made friends with his fellow-slaves and learned the Irish language while waiting for God to tell him what to do next. He had to wait for a long time.

The leaves of the wood marked the seasons, changing from tender lime through green to October gold. When wind and rain lashed the bare winter branches Patrick huddled in his hut, and when spring came he delivered the lambs. His pale skin grew weatherbeaten and his muscles strengthened through hard work. He could have knocked down any of the farmers who had laughed at him the day he landed in Ireland. Six years passed and Patrick was twenty-two when, on a cold September night, he heard a voice speaking clearly in the dark.

"Soon you will be going to your own country," it said, and shortly afterwards added, "Look! Your ship is ready."

3

Running Away

⊗

Although he had waited so long for God's instructions and knew in his heart that they must be obeyed, Patrick was now strangely reluctant to act. Once he would have been overjoyed by the prospect of returning to his own country, but six years on he shrank from it. He knew that Lupita had been carried off into slavery on that terrible spring morning, but had no idea whether or not his parents had escaped the same fate. How heartbreaking it would be to return to the villa at Bannavem Taberniae and find a burnt-out shell, with the salt wind blowing desolately through rooms where a happy family had once lived.

There were practical problems too. It was all very well for God to say, "Your ship is ready," but where was the ship to be found? One bright afternoon Patrick climbed the hill that sheltered the Wood of Foclath from the sea. He had heard it called "the western sea", and realised that Míleac had brought him all the way across Ireland from his landing place in the east.

Looking north and south, Patrick could see mile

after mile of lonely shore, with breakers thundering over jagged rocks and neither ship nor harbour in sight. Before him the sea stretched to the horizon which Patrick believed was the edge of the world. Not even a message from God, he thought with a shudder, would persuade him to sail over that sickening rim. That was when Patrick realised that if he were to return to his own land, he had a long journey on foot ahead of him. He could only sail back from the coast where he had landed.

Then there was Míleac. Although Patrick didn't like being a slave and cruelty towards slaves disgusted him, he didn't believe that owning slaves was wicked. In his day everyone who could afford to did, and Patrick felt that since Míleac had bought him it would be wrong – as well as dangerous – to abscond. But what was he to do? Patrick's father had sometimes freed faithful slaves when they became too old to work, and very occasionally a slave had scraped together enough money to buy his freedom. But Míleac owed Patrick no favour after a mere six years, and Patrick had no money at all.

Patrick did consider briefly going to Míleac and asking for his freedom, but quickly concluded that this was a crazy idea. Míleac was a decent enough man. He didn't beat his slaves and everyone who worked for him had warm clothes and enough to eat. The trouble was that he followed the old religion of the druids; indeed Patrick had heard a rumour that Míleac actually was a druid, and acted out pagan rites deep in the Wood of Foclath. If this were true, it was easy to imagine Míleac's reaction to a request to set Patrick free because the Christian god had work for him to do.

In the end, Patrick accepted that he would have to run away. Still, he felt guilty about breaking his bond with Míleac, and promised himself that one day he would come back and put things right. He didn't like leaving his sheep either, but reminded himself that God too was a shepherd. God would see that no harm came to them.

One moonlit October night, when Míleac and his household were feasting in the great hall and there was the least likelihood that he would be seen, Patrick checked that his sheep were safely folded. Taking his blanket cloak and a small bundle containing apples and some barley cake and cheese which he had saved from his rations, he flitted like a ghost along the border of the wood. He kept under the trees until the glow of the hall and the sound of music and laughter had died away, then he struck out across country, away from the sea.

"The Lord is my shepherd," he reminded himself as the moon vanished behind a cloud and darkness enfolded him. *"I shall not want."*

4

Patrick's Voyage

⠀⠀

Hiding by day and travelling by night until he was many miles from the Wood of Foclath, Patrick went east through brown peat bogs and over wild, brackeny moorland. He was thankful when he felt safe enough to travel in daylight; he didn't know how to read the stars reliably and often got hopelessly lost. Once he was able to orientate himself by the sun things were easier, and he went eastward at a faster pace. His food soon ran out, and as chill November shrivelled the fruits of the countryside he was cold and often hungry.

Sometimes, however, he passed a farm or a lonely cabin where a kind family took pity on him; a meal of mutton broth and a night in the dry straw of the cow's shelter put new heart into him. Next morning he went resolutely on his way. But the fallen leaves and sharpening frosts warned Patrick that winter was at hand, and he felt relief as well as joy when, one misty afternoon, he crested a ridge and saw the rolling grey water of the eastern sea.

Patrick spent that night in a little cave and next

morning set out hopefully along the shore. Soon he came to a village of wattle huts grouped around a rough wooden landing-stage. His heart seemed to miss a beat when he saw a large, sea-going curach with furled sail swaying on the dark water.

"This is it, isn't it?" he said to God, and although he heard no voice he knew that God's answer was "Yes." Which made what happened next as mysterious as it was provoking.

Patrick was aware that he must look terrible. He wondered whether he should go to the water's edge, wash his face and hands and at least try to get some of the mud off his cloak and sandals. But he reckoned that he was now so travel-stained that a wash and brush-up would make little difference. So he ran his fingers through his brown hair and hurried down to the landing-stage. It was just as well that he hadn't wasted time; the anchor was already raised, most of the crew were on board and those still on shore were preparing to loose the mooring rope.

"Hi! Wait a minute," Patrick called as he hurried along the shore. "Have you room for me? I'm strong and I'll gladly work my passage. Please take me along."

The sailors on the landing-stage, nut-brown men with hard, muscular bodies, paused with the ropes between their hands. They had no objection to taking a passenger willing to do some of their work for them. But just as they began to nod and say, "Come aboard, then," the captain leant over the side of the ship.

"No way!" he bawled, wildly waving his hands.

The sailors looked embarrassed, and Patrick gazed in astonishment at the man's scarlet, angry face. He knew he looked like a vagabond, but even that didn't explain why the captain was so excited – frightened, even, to judge by his popping black eyes.

"But – " began Patrick.

The captain interrupted.

"Push off," he yelled. "You're not coming with us."

Patrick was deeply disappointed, but he sensed that there was no point in arguing with someone so unreasonable.

"It's all right," he said politely, using the Irish language that was now so familiar to him that he was forgetting his native tongue. "I'll wait for another ship. Sorry to have troubled you, sir."

He smiled at the sailors who had been willing to take him, nodded and walked away quickly. He didn't want them to see that there were tears in his eyes.

It didn't take long to get back to the cave where he had spent the night. Too fatigued and dispirited to go further, Patrick crawled into it. It all seemed so unfair. He was sure he had travelled two hundred miles from Míleac's farm, and just when he thought God had provided the ship he had promised, everything had gone wrong. Still, praying had become his habit, so as he sat watching the sea swishing and foaming on to the beach, he began to pray.

"Lead me, Lord . . ."

Suddenly Patrick heard a shout.

"Oi! You, young man!"

Poking out his head, he saw one of the sailors he had spoken to earlier waving and scrambling towards him over the loose shingle. Eagerly he scrambled out of the cave.

"What is it?" he gasped. "Has the captain changed his mind?"

The sailor nodded, out of breath.

"He's a funny fellow, our captain," he replied, grinning at Patrick. "Superstitious as they come. First the gods warned him that you were bad luck. Now they've changed their minds and say you're good luck after all. You're to hurry up, or we'll miss the tide. My name's Cairbre, by the way."

"Patrick," smiled Patrick, grasping Cairbre's outstretched hand.

Patrick knew that he had got away from Ireland in the nick of time. Soon the season of storms would come, and ships would be drawn high up on the shore until spring. In some ways the voyage reminded him of the last one he had taken, tied up with other prisoners in the bottom of the pirate ship. The smells of salt and tar were evocative, while the creaking of the rigging and the slap of black water against the sides still got on his landsman's nerves.

But this time everything else was different. Instead of despair Patrick felt hope. Although the crew were all as pagan as their captain, and there had been some black looks when Patrick explained that he was a Christian and couldn't follow their customs, on the whole they got on well. Cairbre introduced Patrick to his friends Fiontán, Aodh and Ailill. They were jolly company for a young man who had spent so much of the last six years alone.

Patrick was kept busy bailing out bilge-water, taking his turn at the oars when the wind dropped, helping to raise the sail and secure the cargo when it suddenly rose. There were dogs on board, great Irish wolfhounds destined to be sold abroad as hunting dogs. Patrick helped to feed them, but soon learned to keep his fingers away from their slavering jaws. They were not friendly animals.

When he was off duty Patrick crouched in the bows, eagerly scanning the horizon for sight of land. Once, through a mist, he thought he glimpsed the island of Monavia which had been visible from the hills above his home. But he wasn't sure, and soon nightfall obscured the view. As he lay wrapped in his cloak, watching stars shining fitfully through rags of cloud, Patrick wondered on which part of the British coast he would land. He hoped fervently that it wouldn't be too far from Bannavem Taberniae. The blisters on his feet from his last long tramp were just beginning to heal and the last thing he wanted was a hike all round Britain.

He hoped in vain, however. During the third night at sea a nasty squall, a foretaste of winter storms, blew the curach badly off course. The dogs howled and the crew called loudly on Manannán, god of the sea, to save them. Patrick, trusting his own god, wasn't afraid, but when next morning land loomed blackly through the dawn mist, he realised that it could be anywhere – the wild shore of Caledonia in the north or the land of the Dumnonii south of the great Sabrina estuary. He soon discovered that no one else on board had a clue either.

5

An Unpleasant Journey

⊗

"I must admit," said Cairbre to Patrick as they tried vainly to shelter under a dismally dripping pine, "that I've often imagined being drowned at sea. It's the risk a sailor runs. But this is the first time I've ever wondered if I'd end my days being eaten by starving wolfhounds. What a life!"

Patrick laughed, but he knew exactly what Cairbre meant. He didn't like the look in the wolfhounds' eyes either.

Days – Patrick wasn't sure how many, but reckoned it might be as long as a month – had passed since the curach, leaking and in need of repair, had run aground on a lonely, rockbound shore. The captain had been cocky.

"Cheer up, lads. This is Roman territory and there's bound to be a town nearby. We'll stock up on food, get the ship mended and be on our way to Gaul in a couple of days. No problem."

So everyone had helped to secure the ship, and Aodh had made leashes for the eight dogs from a coil of rope in the stern. Foolishly, as it turned out, they had eaten the last of their ship's provisions on the shore. Then, with their cloaks already lightly furred with drizzle, the whole crew had begun to trudge inland.

At first there had been quite a lot of singing and joking, but as an eerie grey countryside unfolded, ringed with sinister black mountains, the voices fell silent. The short November day faded without town or village coming into view. By the time the company stopped to spend the night in the poor shelter of a ruined sheepfold, no one was laughing. The captain was a lot less confident.

"Don't look at me like that," he said defensively, although in fact everyone had been avoiding his eye. "There's bound to be at least a village nearby. We'll find it tomorrow, for sure."

"Famous last words," muttered Aodh, and so it had proved.

Day after day the crew and their increasingly ill-tempered dogs journeyed up hill and down dale, struggling through marshes and across icy streams, unable to find a human habitation or to find their way back to the ship. Rain fell incessantly and they were frozen to the marrow. It was a nightmare. On the evening when Cairbre had made his remark about being eaten by dogs they had had nothing but grass and withered berries to eat for days. Two sailors, too weak to continue, had dropped back from the rest, who knew they would never see them again. Ailill had suggested loosing the dogs, but the captain had snarled a refusal.

"Don't be a fool. The dogs are the only valuable things we have. We'll get a fortune for them when we reach Gaul."

No one was brave enough to say, "If we reach Gaul," but Patrick knew it was what they were all thinking. During the last few days he had also sensed a change in their attitude to him. Cairbre remained friendly, but the eyes of others now looked at him resentfully. There were muttered conversations that stopped abruptly when he drew near. On a cold, windy afternoon when the miserable little band arrived at a rock they had passed that morning and realised that they had spent the whole day going round in a circle, anger and discontent boiled over.

"This is your fault, you Christian scum," shouted the captain, glowering at Patrick as if he'd like to kill him. "I knew you were bad luck the minute I set eyes on you. What about this god of yours, eh? If he's so wonderful, why don't you say a prayer and get him to send us something to eat?" And as the rest of the crew, even those who had been Patrick's friends, muttered in sullen agreement, the captain continued with a break in his voice. "We're all going to die of hunger. I don't believe we'll see another human being, ever again."

It was an ugly moment. These men were desperate, and they were armed. Patrick knew that he was in danger, but he also heard the despair in the captain's voice. The man had tried to be a good leader, but now it was all too much for him. Patrick felt sorry for him.

"Look," he said gently, "I will pray. But it would help if you'd all pray to my god too. Nothing's impossible to him, and it's quite probable that this very day he'll send us even more food than we need."

So, not because they believed but because they were at the end of their tether, the crew called on Patrick's god to help them. Everyone except Patrick was dumbfounded when a herd of pigs ran grunting and squealing out of a nearby wood.

For the rest of his life, the smell of roasting pork would remind Patrick of that night in the wilderness. Although some of the pigs managed to escape into the twilight, just as many were captured and efficiently butchered by the starving sailors. Some dry brushwood was found under the trees and a fire started. Aodh enhanced the feast by finding a honeycomb in a hollow tree. After being the least popular person in the party, suddenly Patrick was everybody's best friend. Even when he refused to share the honeycomb which the pagans were offering as a thanksgiving to their gods, no offence was taken. Patrick observed ruefully that it was easy enough to get people to pray to his god when they were starving. Once they were fed, it took them an hour or so to return to their old ways.

The dogs, stuffed with pork, snored loudly by the dying embers of the fire. When they had dried their clothes, the sailors wrapped themselves in their cloaks and quickly fell asleep. Patrick had more difficulty; for a long time he sat apart, hugging his knees and listening to the sighing of the wind in the branches. The rain had stopped and the moon rose, very white and sharp. When eventually Patrick too rolled himself in his cloak and fell asleep, he was sure that God was near.

In the still, icy hour before dawn, Patrick dreamt. It

was another stone dream. This time he thought that an enormous boulder had fallen on top of him, pinning him to the ground. He was paralysed and suffocating under its weight. Then, as he was struggling to take enough air into his lungs to call for help, Patrick saw the sun rise. He wanted to shout, "God! Please help me!" but to his surprise the words that actually came out of his mouth were, "Helias! Helias!"

Immediately the rising sun shot into the sky and shone fiercely down on Patrick. In the heat of the sun's rays the stone on his breast melted, and he was free. But just as he scrambled thankfully to his feet the dream faded and he woke shivering in his damp cloak on the cold ground. Rolling over, Patrick lay frowning up at the leaden sky.

For a while the dream seemed incomprehensible. This annoyed Patrick, who believed that there was meaning in dreams. At last, from far back in his childhood, a memory returned to him. Once, as a small boy, he had gone with his father Calpornius to visit a villa much grander than their own. The owner had been Christian like themselves, and on the wall of his entrance hall Patrick had seen a painting of the Old Testament prophet Elijah, who was also called "Helias", surrounded by the golden rays of the sun. Patrick had forgotten most of what he had learned at school, but he did remember that in Greek a similar word, "helios", meant "the sun". It took him rather longer to work out what the dream might mean.

Eventually he explained it to himself like this: Elijah's task had been to carry God's messages to the kings and people of Israel, who as often as not had taken offence and refused to listen. Patrick guessed that God was warning him that his task would be rather like Elijah's. He wouldn't always be popular, and he would meet lots of people just as truculent as the pagan crew. Still, like Elijah, he must trust in the true God. But what about the sun? In the blank grey morning Patrick had no difficulty in understanding what the sun in his dream had represented. It was the love of God that would keep him warm through all the hardships to come.

Things began to get better now. After a breakfast of cold pork the company set out again. Patrick couldn't help laughing at the sight of the crew crashing through the wild countryside, dragged along by the dogs and laden with enormous cuts of meat. Although it went on raining, everyone's spirits improved; on the tenth day after meeting the pigs they came over a hill and saw below them a wooden-walled town at the estuary of a slow, silver river. Aodh cheered and even the captain's black-browed face wore a sunny smile.

"Why don't you stay with us?" he asked Patrick when they had bartered the remains of their pork for bread, wine, eggs and materials to mend the curach. "We're going to work our way back round the coast to the ship, then we'll be on our way to Gaul. I knew you were good luck the minute I set eyes on you," he added with an effrontery that was amusing and appalling at the same time.

"No, thanks," replied Patrick firmly. "I've had enough of sea voyages to last a lifetime. I'm off home now to see my family."

He smiled as he said it, but inside him his heart sank. He really didn't know whether he had a home or a family any more. He only knew that he had to find out. When he had said goodbye to his friends Patrick left the town and tramped inland towards the great north road.

There was no danger of getting lost now. The roads the Romans had built were straight and well paved, and Patrick made steady progress. He kept a wary eye open for bandits, but saw only other law-abiding folk – a fat merchant lolling in a carriage, an army officer in a chariot, haughty with billowing red cloak and waving helmet plume. Now and then a column of footsore legionaries would slog by with a glum centurion at its head.

As the milestones fell away behind him and cold, pearly weather followed the rain, Patrick couldn't help a surge of optimism. The misty blue hills rising on the northern sky were his hills of home, after all. At the garrison town of Deva he left the main road. By less frequented tracks he pushed on towards Bannavem Taberniae, below the great barrier wall.

6

A Face in the Mirror

Concessa, the wife of Deacon Calpornius, sat slumped in a wicker chair in her bedroom with her bare feet on a stool. Her slave Galla fussed around, fixing her mistress's elaborately piled hair with ivory pins, clasping heavy gold bracelets on her painfully thin wrists.

"There now," said the girl, holding up a silver mirror and moving the lamp so that Concessa could see her reflection. "Have I done well?"

Concessa pursed her lips ruefully as she studied her own face. She had been seriously ill after her children had been abducted by pirates in a raid six years ago, and had never recovered her health or her looks. Her dark eyes were sunken and her hair was prematurely grey, while deep lines on her forehead and around her mouth made her look much older than forty-three. Her appearance depressed Concessa, but she didn't want to hurt Galla, who was a well-meaning girl.

"You've done all you can," she said, kindly if non-committally. "Now go and see if my husband is in his

25

room. I think I heard his footsteps in the hall a moment ago."

She heard the anxiety in her own voice and felt impatient with herself. She knew it was absurd to panic every time Calpornius was a few minutes late back from a council meeting in town, but since Sucat and Lupita were taken she could scarcely bear to let him out of her sight.

Galla put down the mirror on the marble-topped dressing table and went out into the dimly-lit entrance hall. A moment later she returned with a puzzled expression on her sallow face.

"My master isn't in his room, lady," she said, "and there's no light in the bath-house."

Concessa shrugged her thin shoulders.

"So I made a mistake," she said. "Go and have your dinner, Galla. I'll wait here till my husband comes."

Galla turned and went slowly back to the hall. She stood for a moment looking thoughtfully into the shadowy corners behind the pillars, but no one was visible, which was odd, because she could have sworn she had heard footsteps too.

Left alone with nothing to do until Calpornius came home to dinner, Concessa sat in front of her dressing table. Fretfully she fingered her combs and scent bottles, brooches, necklets and rings. As always when she was alone, her thoughts turned to her lost children. Were they dead or alive, she wondered. If they were alive, where were they now? Did they ever think of her? Concessa tortured herself endlessly with unanswerable questions, and tears of self-pity flooded her brown eyes at the thought that Sucat and Lupita might have forgotten their mother.

Concessa wasn't really concentrating as she picked up her silver hand-mirror and again glanced at her haggard face. But it wasn't the pallor of her complexion that made her eyes dilate and her throat contract with terror. Behind her, also reflected, Concessa saw a barbarian standing in the doorway. He was very tall, with wild hair, a thick brown beard and a filthy, tattered cloak. God have mercy, Concessa thought. I did hear footsteps, of an Irish pirate. The raiders have come again. The mirror fell from her shaking hand as she turned to face him – only because, absurdly, it seemed preferable to being attacked from behind. Breathlessly but bravely she attempted defiance.

"How dare you try to force your way in here? My husband – "

But a voice she knew interrupted her as the barbarian held out his empty hands.

"Mother, don't be frightened. It's me, Sucat."

Before Concessa could move or speak he had leapt across the floor and taken her in his arms.

That night, bathed, shaved and well fed, Patrick slept soundly under clean blankets. His grief and shock at his parents' changed appearance had been softened by delight at their happiness; over a long dinner he had told his traveller's tales, basking in the warmth of their admiration of his courage and resourcefulness. Even the absence of Lupita hadn't shadowed his homecoming, since Calpornius said stoutly that if one miracle could happen, why not two?

Next morning Patrick accompanied his father round the farm in the winter sunshine. Although he had rebuilt the villa after the raid, Calpornius had allowed the farm to go to ruin. Weedy fields, tumbledown barns and burnt-out cottages told the sad story of a man who had suddenly stopped having a purpose in life.

"What happened to Dion?" asked Patrick, staring sombrely at the shell of the house where his friend used to live.

"Taken with his father, mother and sisters," replied Calpornius sadly. "Nearly all our people were torn from us that dreadful day. How your mother and I escaped, I'll never know."

"I wish I hadn't been so high and mighty with him," said Patrick, but his father wasn't listening.

"With your mother so ill, I'm afraid I let things go," he admitted. But then he straightened his rounded shoulders and added cheerfully, "Never mind. It will be different now that you're home. We'll hire labour in town, buy some animals and seed corn, rebuild the village . . ."

Patrick allowed him to rattle on, concealing the unease this planning caused him. It would be cruel, he told himself, to announce so soon to his happy parents that he was here on a visit, not home for good.

As the days passed, however, and a new year struggled towards spring, Patrick still delayed sharing with his parents his plans for the future. He didn't forget God, but little by little he fell back into the habits of a wealthy Romano-British youth. He rose late and breakfasted well before riding out with his father.

In the afternoon he played board games with his mother, then rested before bathing and consuming an enormous evening meal. When he felt guilty he reminded himself that he had a duty to his invalid mother; Concessa was still very frail, and if he were to leave her suddenly the shock would probably kill her. All the same, Patrick often felt that God was nudging his elbow, and he knew that quite soon the most painful choice of his life would have to be made.

The crisis came one night in May, when sheep were calling to their lambs on the hill and the hawthorn outside Patrick's window was a foaming torrent of scented blossom. No sooner had he fallen asleep than he began to dream.

Patrick hadn't made many close friends when he worked as a slave for Míleac mac Boin. One young man he had liked a lot was called Victoricus. The last time Patrick had seen him, Victoricus had been grooming a horse in Míleac's stable yard. Now, in the dream, he was standing facing Patrick and with his back to the Wood of Foclath. In each hand Victoricus held a thick bundle of letters which Patrick somehow knew were addressed to him. When he held out his hand Victoricus stepped forward and handed him one of them; Patrick saw that its heading was, "The Voice of the Irish". He had just begun to read it when his eye was caught by movement in the wood. Suddenly it seemed that all the people of Ireland were under the trees behind Victoricus, holding out their hands to him. Patrick heard their voices raised in one longing cry.

"Holy boy, we ask you to come and walk among us once again."

Holy boy. When he woke in the fragile dawn light, Patrick didn't know whether to laugh or cry. Whatever else he was, he wasn't a holy boy. He had wasted the chance of a good education, he had been thoughtless and arrogant towards less privileged children, and he had once done something so shameful that he had never spoken of it to a living soul.

Patrick knew that he had improved a bit during his time as a slave, when he had talked to God and learned to trust him, and he had never forgotten the dream where God had picked up the stone and put it on top of the wall. He supposed too that he had acquitted himself quite well during his journey across Ireland, and in the fearful days he had spent with the sailors and their dogs. But the minute he had got home he had started enjoying luxury again, eating and drinking too much, being imperious with the servants and fretting about the cut of his clothes. Holy boy! That was a good one. And yet . . .

As the pure, sweet note of a blackbird pierced the morning, Patrick accepted how things had to be. God was calling him to return to Ireland and preach the Gospel, and he dared not disobey. But when he thought of breaking the news to Calpornius and Concessa, he could scarcely bear it. Burying his head in his pillow, Patrick sobbed bitterly.

7

A Miracle Remembered

⊗

At the beginning, it was all just as ghastly as Patrick had thought it would be. Unable to find eloquence, he stammered through his story, angrily realising that it must sound even less convincing to Calpornius and Concessa than it did to him. Their reaction was predictably violent. Like a small child whose stubborn wrongdoing had finally fractured his parents' patience, Patrick stood hunched while waves of bewilderment and hostility broke over him. Concessa sobbed hysterically.

"How can you suggest such a thing, after all you've suffered already in that terrible country? Are you mad? Are you utterly selfish? Sucat, you're all we have left."

Calpornius blustered, his sagging face going red and white by turns.

"I always knew you weren't bright, but for sheer stupidity this beats all. After all we've done for you! How dare you upset your mother like this when you know how ill she's been?"

Patrick resented this emotional blackmail, but he

had no defence against it. He remembered something in the Gospel about Christ's yoke being easy and his burden light. Not at a time like this, it isn't, thought Patrick bitterly.

Then Concessa took to her bed and stayed there for a week, refusing to see Patrick. He was further pained by the reproachful looks of Galla and the other servants.

"I'm your master's son," he wanted to snarl. "Don't dare to look at me like that."

Then he felt horrified and ashamed.

Eventually Patrick started going into the hills in the morning and staying out all day. But wandering by the streams and staring at the blue vistas brought him no solace. His mind was too turbulent to seek God's silence, and it was agonising to know that he was seeing this dear landscape for the last time. For in spite of everything he was holding firm to his intention. There was nothing else he could do.

In the end, as usually happens, the storm blew itself out. One evening Concessa appeared at dinner looking exhausted but calm. Little was said as the family reclined round the table eating eggs, oysters and green salad, but Patrick sensed that the atmosphere had changed.

It had been a beautiful day, and at the end of the meal Concessa suggested that they should take their dessert and the last of the wine into the little paved courtyard at the heart of the house. Calpornius carried out the wine and a dish of dried fruit, while Patrick helped his mother into a chair and tucked a rug around her knees. Again there was silence while

Calpornius watered the terracotta herb pots in the alcoves round the walls. When he had finished he came to join Patrick on a stone bench.

"Well now," said Calpornius gruffly. "I think it's time we had a talk, boy. Your mother and I can't pretend we're happy, but we see you'll go whatever we say. The one thing we couldn't bear would be to part from you in anger. So you'd better tell us what you have in mind and we'll see what we can do to help."

Patrick knew what this generosity was costing, and his heart ached. But he reckoned it was better to answer matter-of-factly.

"I'll have to study for a while," he told his father. "I never worked at school and I'm a complete ignoramus. If I went back to Ireland now and set myself up as a preacher, everyone would laugh at me."

Calpornius didn't contradict him.

"Would you like to go to Rome?" he asked.

Although he had never travelled further than Eburacum, as a Roman citizen Calpornius had always thought of Rome as a jewel set in the forehead of the world. Patrick shook his head uncertainly.

"Maybe, eventually," he said. "What I'd really like would be to go to the monastery on the island of Aralensis, off the south coast of Gaul. The abbot's Honoratus, a famous teacher and holy man. I'd be happy to join his community for a while, if he'd have me. Maybe after a few years I could be a deacon like you, Father."

This sly compliment misfired. Calpornius burst out laughing.

"Son," he said frankly, "I'm sure you know I only

became a deacon to avoid collecting taxes – one of the more tedious aspects of my job as a government official. Churchmen don't have to collect taxes. No one would ever call me a devout man. Yet I can't stand between another man and his conscience, even if that man is my only son. I'll write to this Abbot Honoratus and ask if he'll have you as a pupil. If he agrees, you'll travel to Aralensis at my expense."

The sudden chill of the northern twilight drove the family indoors. Later, as Patrick was passing his mother's bedroom door, he heard her voice.

"Sucat!"

Patrick went in. Concessa was in bed, looking oddly girlish with her grey hair in a plait over her shoulder. She patted the striped bedspread. Patrick went and sat beside her.

"Mother," he began, "I don't know how to thank you," but Concessa stopped him with an impatient movement of her hand.

"I want to tell you something," she said, her dark eyes huge in the lamplight. "I've kept thinking about it, and it's what has made me change my mind about – about what you want to do." Patrick waited, and after a slight hesitation Concessa went on. "Sucat, do you remember a day when you were a little boy and Lupita had an accident in the cornfield?"

Patrick frowned.

"Vaguely," he said.

"Yes." Concessa nodded. "You couldn't have been more than seven. Some children came running to the gate, screaming that Lupita had fallen on a rusty ploughshare. They said she had cut her chest and was bleeding badly. Your father went to fetch her, and when they came back I nearly fainted with terror. There was a great gash on Lupita's chest, about a hand's length, and your father's tunic was drenched in blood. Father said he would ride to town and fetch a surgeon, but the child was barely conscious and I really thought she might die before he returned."

"And?" whispered Patrick.

"While I was sitting by Lupita trying to staunch the blood," said Concessa, "you came into the room. For a moment you stood watching us, then you came forward and said, 'Don't worry, Mother.' You touched the wound."

There was a tensely silent moment, then Patrick said hoarsely, "I remember now. I healed her."

"Yes. By the time the surgeon arrived the blood had stopped flowing, and where the gash had been there was only a thin scar. He wasn't best pleased with us, I remember." Concessa smiled tremulously, but when she spoke again her voice was steady. "That's why I'm learning to make sense of what's happening now," she said. "For all that you were such a wild, lazy scamp in your teens, I suppose I've always known you weren't an ordinary boy. I only wish you were."

Patrick didn't know what to say. He kissed his mother and went thoughtfully to bed.

Of course, the actual leaving was heartbreaking. It couldn't be any other way. Believing that God has taken a hand in one's affairs doesn't provide immunity from suffering, and Patrick's last days at home were poignant beyond tears.

On the morning of his departure, when he came out into the frosty courtyard wearing the new tunic and goat's wool travelling cloak which his mother had provided, Patrick's eyelids burned and the words he wanted to say stuck in his aching throat. In silence he embraced his parents, mounted the horse his father had given him and rode stiffly along the track. On the brow of the hill he turned and raised his hand, but there was no one to return his wave. The gate was closed, and Patrick knew that his parents hadn't been able to endure watching him go.

8

One Step on the Road

❄

The island of Aralensis, where Patrick arrived in late
autumn, was not at all the kind of place he had
imagined. His dream of a monastery where a kindly
abbot would help him with his studies, and where he
would have the encouragement of his fellow-students,
didn't survive the first twenty-four hours. On the long,
lonely journey down through Gaul, Patrick had looked
forward to being a member of a community. Aralensis
didn't seem to him like a community at all.

Abbot Honoratus, who met Patrick on the shore,
was a crabby old man in a tattered robe. He had dirty
feet and grey lice in his straggling beard. It was obvious
that he considered the other Christians who had
settled on the island pests, and ruled them harshly.
They were forbidden to talk to each other and
crouched mumbling prayers in their narrow,
comfortless cells. Patrick soon learned that swift
punishment followed any breaking of Abbot
Honoratus's rules.

In fact the starvation diet, hours of night prayer and

sleeping on the hard ground didn't bother Patrick. He had endured conditions just as bad as Míleac's slave. It was the course of study decreed by Honoratus that reduced him to despair. Only his burning ambition to return to Ireland prevented him from running away at the end of the first month.

"O God, be not far from me: O my God, make haste to help me," he pleaded feverishly, as he sat surrounded by the handwritten books and scrolls which Honoratus had lent him. But as he struggled to remember what Augustine had said about this and Origen had said about that, he sometimes felt that the God he had once known so well was hiding his face from him.

By the spring, things had become so bad that Patrick decided he would have to start again somewhere else. After a long, frustrating round of other monasteries in the Mediterranean area, he found himself in another autumn and again on the road. This time on foot and little better than a beggar, Patrick tramped in the rain up the busy highway. He was aware as never before of the lawlessness that was sweeping away the ordered world. He would have been attacked and robbed by bandits if they had thought he had anything worth stealing; as it was, he saw beatings and robberies which sickened him but which he was powerless to prevent. By day the road was thronged with hard-faced legionaries on the march south; Patrick learned with sinking heart that many of them were from Britain. The army was withdrawing from the north, and the great Roman peace was finally at an end.

At long last, on a grey winter afternoon, Patrick

reached the gate of the church at Autissiodorum in northern Gaul. It was to be his home for some years to come.

"The thing to remember about study," said Bishop Germanus as he and Patrick made a round of the garden before evening prayer, "is that it shouldn't be rushed – especially if you return to it after many years away. I'll direct your studies, but you must set your own pace. Once you stop worrying about forgetting, you'll be astonished how your memory improves."

These words were balm to Patrick. He had been overjoyed by his kindly reception. Everything inside the sturdy stockade delighted him – the wooden church surrounded by dining-room, kitchen, library, mill and guest-house, and beyond the garden a village of wattle huts. These sheltered the priests, deacons and students who made up the community. Germanus, a lean man with greying hair and clear blue eyes, had greeted Patrick with a warmth the young man could hardly credit after his stay with the austere Honoratus. Relief made Patrick impetuous.

"Sir," he blurted out eagerly, "how soon do you suppose I can become a deacon?"

Germanus, who had stooped to rescue an earthworm that had got itself stranded on the path, straightened up and lifted his eyebrows.

"What's the hurry?" he asked lightly.

Patrick flushed. He had been on the point of telling this distinguished churchman about the dream in which the people of Ireland had called to him, but suddenly it didn't seem a good idea after all. Too like boasting on his first day at a new school. All the same, he thought he might as well mention his ambition.

"I was a slave in Ireland," he said. "One day I'd like to carry the Gospel into that land."

In the fading light Patrick found Germanus's face hard to read, and he received only a grunt in reply. But he was left with the impression that as the Roman world disintegrated outside the gates of Autissiodorum, evangelising Ireland wasn't high on the bishop's list of priorities.

As weeks became months and months years, however, Patrick found happiness of a kind at Autissiodorum. Bishop Germanus had been right. Once he relaxed his concentration improved, and so did his memory. Patrick would never have a true scholar's patience and love of learning, but by hard work he acquired the knowledge of the Bible and other religious books that meant so much to him. Once back in Ireland, he would be able to stand his ground. Although close friendships were discouraged at Autissiodorum too, the atmosphere among the clergy and students was cordial. One young deacon, Amicus, was particularly kind and helpful.

At long last the time approached when Patrick, still strong and healthy but no longer in his first youth, was ready to take the first step towards the priesthood. On Easter Day, along with half a dozen other students, he would be ordained deacon by Bishop Germanus. It ought to have been a happy time, but Patrick was worried – so worried that as the ceremony approached he really wondered whether he could go through with it.

The problem was that Patrick had a guilty secret.

Many years ago, when he had lived at Bannavem Taberniae as an unruly schoolboy, he had done something bad – so bad that for months he had lived in terror of his parents' finding out. When this hadn't happened, he had buried the memory deeply and had never mentioned the incident to a living soul. He had recalled it in agony on the night when he heard the Irish people calling him a holy boy, but then had managed to forget again.

Now, as the day of his ordination approached, the memory resurfaced to torment Patrick. Ought someone who had even once behaved so badly become a deacon, he wondered. Was he fit to be a minister of God? Never had Patrick so deeply desired to hear a voice assuring him of God's forgiveness, but God was silent on the subject. Patrick couldn't sleep and he lost a lot of weight.

Afterwards Patrick would wish fervently that he had taken his problem to Bishop Germanus, and he might have done so had he not one afternoon run into Deacon Amicus in the garden. It was raining, and Patrick was hurrying to get to his cell before his cloak and shoes were soaked. He felt rather impatient when Amicus took him by the sleeve and drew him firmly into the shelter of the church porch. Amicus was Patrick's senior, however, and Patrick owed him obedience and respect.

"How can I help you, brother?" he asked politely.

Amicus snorted softly as he twitched Patrick's hood back from his face. His brown eyes looked keenly into Patrick's grey ones.

"I think you're the one needing help, brother," he replied candidly. "You don't eat and you look like a shadow of your old self. Why don't you come into the church and tell me what's the matter? You know I'll help if I can."

It was so kindly and solicitously said that Patrick was completely disarmed. God has sent Amicus to help me, he thought as he stepped into the dark, draughty interior where the sanctuary lamp shone like a single star. There in the shadows he whispered into Amicus's ear the story he had thought he could never tell anyone.

"I'm not fit to be a deacon," he concluded, straining his eyes to see the expression on Amicus's round face.

He desperately wanted to be contradicted.

Amicus was silent for a moment, then he said gently, "Listen, brother. If we are truly sorry, God will forgive our sins and blot them out. I can see that you've suffered for yours, and so can God. There's no reason why something that happened when you were fifteen should prevent your becoming a deacon now."

A great wave of relief and joy broke over Patrick. He was so grateful that it didn't even occur to him to ask Amicus to keep his secret.

Late in the evening of Easter Day, when he could still feel the kind pressure of Bishop Germanus's hands on his head, Patrick sat down in his cell to write a letter home. As lamplight flickered around the mud-daubed walls, he poured out to his parents the story of his great day. Only as he reached the end did anxiety cloud his pleasure.

For many years Patrick had written home regularly, and letters from his parents had found their way to him in Gaul. They were brave, loving letters, telling him that the apples were ripening, that Uncle Marcus had been to stay, that Galla had become like a daughter to them in their old age. They never mentioned Lupita, and Patrick knew that they had abandoned hope of the new miracle that would bring their real daughter home.

Now, as he folded up his letter, it occurred to Patrick that he hadn't heard from his parents for nearly a year. Biting his lip, he spread out the page again and wrote, "Please, reply soon." But that year was to pass, then another and another, and still no word would come. At last, with a heavy heart, Patrick stopped writing too.

He was never to know whether Calpornius and Concessa had died peacefully, or whether they were sucked into chaos as marauding Caledonian tribes broke through the deserted Roman wall. He went on praying for their safety long after he knew in his heart that they were no more.

9

A False Friend

⊗

When he decided to become a cleric, Patrick knew that he would have to give up many things. The days were past when men like his grandfather and father were allowed to combine office in the church with marriage and a career. Patrick was aware that he would never have a home of his own, a wife and children, wealth or worldly success. Because he loved God he accepted these privations gladly, but there was one restriction he found very hard to bear. This was that he was no longer free to plan his own life as he wished. Although he wasn't a monk, Patrick knew that he couldn't leave Autissiodorum and return to Ireland without the backing of the bishops of Gaul and Britain.

After yet more years of study, when his brown hair was beginning to turn grey, Patrick was ordained priest. His head was tonsured and he began to say Mass daily in the church. He hoped that Bishop Germanus might take a decision about his future, but Germanus, now on the threshold of old age, gave no sign that he had any task in mind for Patrick. Then, quite suddenly, things began to change.

The first excitement was that Bishop Germanus announced that he was going to Britain, and would be away for several weeks.

"There is trouble in the British church," he told the community after evening prayer. "Some of our fellow-Christians there are turning away from the true faith. I have been asked by Pope Celestine to go and help sort the problem out. I shall be taking Father Amicus with me as my chaplain and Father Martin will be in charge here while I am away."

As the fathers and brothers filed out into the mellow summer evening, there was a faint buzz of forbidden conversation. In a life so predictable and humdrum, any event out of the ordinary was a pleasant diversion. Patrick was making for his cell and a stint of reading while daylight lasted when Father Amicus caught up with him. His round face was pink with delight.

"Father Patrick," he said, fairly skipping along at Patrick's side between the bean rows. "I've got something to tell you that will really make your heart glad."

Patrick couldn't help looking affectionately at his companion. He had never forgotten his debt to Amicus, and greatly admired his constant kindness and good-humour. Amicus would be missed during his absence in Britain, but no one would grudge him the honour Bishop Germanus was bestowing on him.

"Tell me, then," Patrick said.

Father Amicus leant against the fence outside Patrick's cell and hitched up his tunic. He glanced round to make sure no one was within earshot, then said, "Listen. It's an open secret that you want to go and preach the Gospel in Ireland. Right?" Patrick nodded. Whenever Ireland was mentioned, his longing was like a sharp pain. "Well then," smiled Amicus, "perhaps you're going to get your chance, my friend."

Patrick's grey eyes widened in amazement.

"How so?" he gasped.

"When we get to Britain," Amicus told him, "there's going to be a synod – a meeting to decide how to set things right in the church there. But also on on the agenda is whether a bishop to the Irish should be appointed. Bishop Germanus has never been keen, but now he's decided it might be good to have someone who'll preach the truth and stop heresy spreading from Britain."

Patrick clutched at his wildly beating chest.

"And – do you suppose – they might choose me?" he whispered hoarsely.

Amicus nodded encouragingly.

"I can't say for sure, of course," he replied, "but I've told Bishop Germanus how keen you are. And if I get a chance to speak at the synod, you can rely on me to put in a good word for you."

Patrick's gratitude was beyond words. What a wonderful friend, he thought. He grasped Amicus's hand tightly, then disappeared into his cell.

As rust began to border the dusty summer leaves and the swallows departed south, the days of Germanus's absence seemed very long to Patrick. He helped to gather the fruit harvest and did his best to concentrate on work and prayer, but the woods and green swards of Ireland swam constantly before his eyes. He recalled his long-ago dream as if it were yesterday, and the imploring voice of the Irish people saying, "Holy boy, we ask you to come and walk among us once again."

Patrick wasn't a boy now. His tanned face was lined and the hair around his tonsure was laced with grey. He was middle-aged, and at a time when plague and hardship cut short many lives, he was feverishly impatient to get on with his.

At long last, in the twinkling dusk of a late October day, Bishop Germanus and his chaplain came riding in at the gate. After supper, word was brought to Patrick that the bishop wished to see him in his cell. This is it, thought Patrick excitedly as he hurried with his lamp through the velvety night.

Bishop Germanus's cell was set apart from the rest. Though chilly and spartan, it was bigger and rather better furnished. When the old man saw Patrick's shadow fall across the floor, he turned on his stool and held out his hand.

"Come here, my son," he said.

"Yes, Father."

Tense with desire and expectation, Patrick went and knelt beside Germanus. But at the bishop's first words all his hope and joy drained swiftly away.

"Patrick, before you were ordained deacon – would it not have been wiser to confess to me the sin of your youth?"

Patrick's mouth went dry and his head spun. For a dreadful moment he thought he was going to keel over in a faint. Somehow he kept upright, though he had to clench his hands tightly to stop them trembling.

"Father Amicus?" he said thickly, then with a cry of pain, "I thought he was my friend!"

Bishop Germanus didn't press for an answer to his question. Sadly but gently, he told Patrick what had happened at the synod in Britain. The matter of the Irish bishopric had been raised, and Patrick's name had been mentioned with approval. But just as the appointment was about to be agreed, Father Amicus had risen to his feet.

"I was surprised," admitted Germanus. "Before we left he had pressed your case with great enthusiasm. But after hearing what he said, my son, I'm afraid the synod changed its mind. I don't myself hold a sin of thirty years ago against you, though I do wish you had confided in me. But others don't know you as well as I do. Palladius of Rome has been appointed bishop. He will leave for Ireland in the spring."

With his hope in tatters and shaking with grief, Patrick left Germanus's cell and stumbled through the dark towards his own. He scarcely noticed when a figure slid from the shadow of the church, but a thin, plaintive voice brought him suddenly to a standstill.

"I'm not to blame. I only followed my conscience, you know."

For once, Patrick's natural politeness deserted him.

"Get out of my way, you Judas," he snarled savagely.

10

Towards Ireland

❈

Wet and dreary, the year dragged on towards its end. Just before Christmas the rain stopped and the wind died down. Overnight a blizzard came spinning out of the north, blanking out the countryside and drifting like wool against the monastery fence. In the freeze that followed, the sun sparkled on the frost-embroidered garden and the white hats on the roofs dripped icicles like long grey hair. The students slid and snowballed a lot when they thought their seniors weren't looking, but Patrick turned a blind eye. A black hood of depression had fallen over him when Germanus and Amicus returned from Britain and he felt that nothing mattered any more.

Despairingly Patrick reviewed his life. In the dark hours, huddling in the remains of the goat's wool cloak his mother had given him so long ago, anger and humiliation kept him from sleep. The thought of the members of the synod wagging their beards, whispering to one another that such a wicked man should never have been ordained, was torture to him.

Even a dream in which he heard God's voice expressing anger at seeing his chosen one stripped of honour didn't comfort him as it ought to have done. Shivering in his freezing little hut, Patrick tried to read and pray, but in vain. He was afraid that he would rot in Autissiodorum for the rest of his life. God and Germanus, however, had other plans.

On a pleasant April afternoon, when the apple trees were in bud and the spring planting had begun, a tall man on a grey horse came riding into the yard. He was plainly dressed in a dark tunic and a long hooded cloak, but his pale, handsome face and dignified air distinguished him from the untidy retinue clattering at his heels. Patrick, on his way from the church to the library, would have looked at him with more interest if he had known who he was, but it wasn't until supper time that he heard someone whispering across the table.

"That's Bishop Palladius. He's spending the night in our guest-house on his way to Ireland from Rome."

As he ate his salted fish and barley bread, Patrick glanced sidelong at Palladius, seated in the place of honour at Germanus's side. He had a choking sensation and turned his head away from the flickering oil lamp on the table. He was afraid that pique and envy would be written on his face for everyone to see.

After supper, the two bishops disappeared to Germanus's cell, and Patrick didn't see Palladius again. Next morning, however, Germanus sent for Patrick. The bishop came quickly to the point.

"My son, I've been giving much thought and prayer to your future, and now I have a proposal for you. Bishop Palladius agrees with me that something you

did so long ago, before you even became a committed
Christian, shouldn't be allowed to spoil your whole life
and deprive the Church of your service. Bishop
Palladius is going to need helpers in Ireland, and we've
agreed that you should be one of them." He sighed and
added ruefully, "I know it isn't what you hoped for,
Patrick, but it's the best we can do."

Patrick could scarcely contain his joy. He looked at
Bishop Germanus with shining eyes.

"Father," he said earnestly, "I only want to go back
to Ireland. Once I'm there, God will direct my path."

Germanus nodded approvingly.

"Good. Then you will leave in September," he
decreed. "Father Segitius will accompany you. God go
with you, my son."

The last weeks at Autissiodorum were happy ones for
Patrick. He could say honestly that being a bishop
mattered a great deal less to him than getting back to
Ireland. On a crisp autumn morning he said goodbye
to his friends and knelt to receive Bishop Germanus's
blessing. Then, with Father Segitius at his side, he rode
away north.

"We should get as far as Eburobrica before sunset,"
said Patrick, adding nostalgically, "I stayed there years
and years ago, on my way to Aralensis from my home
in Britain."

"I'm a Gaul myself," replied Segitius dolefully.
"Never been to sea in my life. Don't fancy it much, to
tell you the truth."

Patrick, who was on top of the world, couldn't help
laughing.

"You'll enjoy it," he said confidently. "We're going to have a wonderful voyage."

It was a pleasant ride up the old Roman road, between fields that had once rippled with ripe grain but were now rapidly returning to wilderness. There were few travellers; the tribal warfare that had ravaged Europe since the withdrawal of the legions still continued, but at present the drift of terror was in another direction. Afterwards Patrick remembered only one figure, a white-faced young man spurring south on a sweating black mare.

Eburobrica, a faded garrison town which Patrick recalled clanking with armour and loud with commerce, now dozed in the mellow warmth of late afternoon. The gatekeeper admitted the two clerics without question, and directed them to the little church below the wall. As he tethered his horse in the dusty courtyard, patting its nose and promising it supper soon, Patrick could never have imagined the shock that awaited him. The elderly priest obviously had no notion how startling his news was; as he showed Patrick and Segitius to the guest-house he spoke quite casually.

"Such a shame about Bishop Palladius. Dead, and such a short time into his mission. Didn't you meet the messenger? He passed through Eburobrica this morning on his way to Rome."

And having invited his guests to join him for supper after evening prayers, he shuffled calmly away to gather some pears from his little garden.

Patrick and Segitius stared at each other in the gloomy little room. Patrick licked his dry lips.

"What do we do next?" he whispered, too stunned to think for himself.

Segitius was in no doubt.

"I think your hour has come, Patrick," he said. "Nothing can prevent your becoming a bishop in Ireland now. We must return to Autissiodorum in the morning so that you can be ordained."

11

The First Convert

❈

The curach carrying Bishop Patrick cut swiftly through
the grey sea, as if it shared his eagerness to reach
Ireland. His companions moaned and complained
about seasickness, but Patrick scarcely noticed. As the
sail puffed before the wind he sat in the creaking bows,
tasting salt on his lips and straining his eyes for the
first glimpse of the Irish coast. Though still overawed
by unexpected events, he had never been so happy in
his life.

Of course, nothing had happened quickly enough
to please Patrick. There had been a long delay while
Germanus contacted other bishops, but at last
everyone agreed to Patrick's ordination. Now, almost a
year after he first set out, he was a man in a hurry.
After four days and nights at sea the curach reached
the port of Inbhear Dé, but Patrick stopped only long
enough for the crew to take on fresh water and food.

"Before I do anything else," he told his assistants
Auxilius and Iserninus, "I have a visit to make. Many
years ago, when I was a slave, I ran away from my

master Míleac. I must return to the Wood of Foclath and repay him the money he lost by my escape."

"Míleac may be dead," pointed out Iserninus, a tall, youngish man with a fringe of red hair around his tonsure.

Patrick shook his head. Somehow he felt sure that Míleac, who hadn't been more than thirty when they last met, was still alive.

"Do you have money, Bishop Patrick?" asked moon-faced Auxilius inquisitively.

"If I hadn't," replied Patrick mildly, "I wouldn't be going, would I?"

He sensed criticism, but he had no intention of telling Auxilius his secret. A quarter of a century ago, when he had sold his horse before crossing into Gaul, he had sewn the gold coins he had received for it into the seam of his goat's wool cloak. Although the cloak had eventually become too ragged to wear, for his mother's sake Patrick wouldn't part with it. It was bundled up under one of the rowing benches now, with Patrick's debt to Míleac safely hidden in its folds. Auxilius pursed his small mouth and lifted his eyebrows a fraction, but Patrick ignored him. From now on, he would be answerable only to God.

For the next week, in bright October weather, Patrick sailed north. Sitting alone in the prow of the curach, he couldn't keep his eyes off the coast of his adopted country. He admired everything – the rocky coves and sudden peninsulas, the green hills beyond, the sea swishing on to pale sand in foamy turquoise coils. Eager as he was to start work, he couldn't help an end-of-holiday feeling when the curach at last rounded a point and slipped into a great sea-lough. The crew found a mooring in the lee of an island and Patrick disembarked on the western shore. It was late afternoon.

"We'll walk while daylight lasts," Patrick told Auxilius, Iserninus and Odhrán, an Irish crewman who was Christian and had asked to come with him. "At sundown we'll look for somewhere to spend the night."

He meant a copse or a hollow in the hills, and his companions understood this. They had all slept in ditches in their time. Obediently each lifted part of the food supply, and with Patrick at their head began to trudge inland. The sun sank crimson behind the mountains and mist rose like smoke around sandalled feet. It was going to be a cold night.

"I do think, Bishop Patrick, that we should be looking for somewhere to sleep," remarked Auxilius as twilight came and Patrick was still striding on. "Before we find ourselves up to our ears in a bog," he added emphatically.

Patrick grinned. It was already clear that Auxilius would never be slow to express an opinion.

"Yes, all right," he agreed, but couldn't resist saying teasingly, "I mustn't let you wear out your feet today, Auxilius. We have two hundred miles between us and the Wood of Foclath."

Laughing at Auxilius's appalled expression, Patrick led the way towards an overhanging rock.

"Do you ever get the feeling that there are eyes watching you?" asked Iserninus when they had finished their supper of apples and cheese and were trying to make themselves comfortable.

He glanced nervously in the direction of a little oakwood that straggled over the brow of a nearby hill.

"It isn't just a feeling," replied Odhrán laconically. "A man's been peeping out at us all the time we've been eating. A fierce-looking wee fellow with straw in his hair."

Patrick's assistants exchanged nervous glances and Auxilius said, "Er, perhaps – oughtn't one of us to go and – um, challenge him?"

"Too late," shrugged Odhrán. "He's gone. Probably to fetch his knife. I think I'll turn in now."

He rolled on to his side, yanked up his cloak and closed his eyes. Patrick laughed softly. He was beginning to like Odhrán.

The joke about the knife misfired, however. As the full moon rose and owls began to hoot eerily in the wood, there was the sudden crack of a twig snapping underfoot. As Patrick and Odhrán leapt to their feet a tall, athletic figure pounced into the open from the trees. Someone small scuttled at his heels.

"Who's there?" demanded the tall man in a gruff voice.

"Friends, who come in the name of the true God," Patrick replied.

"And are about to be murdered," whispered Auxilius, cowering under his cloak.

As if to prove him right there was an unpleasant, rasping sound of a knife being drawn from its sheath. It gleamed coldly as the stranger advanced.

"We are unarmed," said Patrick steadfastly, "and we come in peace. Will you kill us in cold blood?"

There was a horrible silence while Odhrán clenched his enormous fists and the assistants held their breath. Then something strange happened. The blade was within centimetres of Patrick's throat and Odhrán was poised to spring when the man holding the weapon seemed to freeze. In the white light he stared into Patrick's eyes and Patrick stared into his. The knife fell to the ground. As Patrick stooped to pick it up, its owner rubbed his eyes.

"My name is Díchú," he said. "My swineherd thought you were robbers and came to warn me. I came to kill you, but –" He shook his head with a bemused smile. "What I really want is to ask you to stay at my house tonight. Will you come? It's just over the hill."

Instead of sleeping uncomfortably on the frosty turf, Auxilius, Iserninus and Odhrán passed the night snugly in Díchú's barn with sheepskins to keep them warm. Patrick eventually joined them, but not until he had spent long hours sitting over the fire with Díchú, telling him about God and his love for Ireland. As dawn broke and the stars faded, the farmer decided to turn his back on the old pagan religion and become a Christian.

At Díchú's invitation, Patrick and his companions stayed on for a day or two, then Patrick decided that it was time to be on his way. On the morning of his departure Díchú said, "I want to give you a present."

"No need," said Patrick, slightly alarmed.

The thought of travelling with a pig or a sheep or even a dog didn't appeal to him. He had travelled with dogs once before. But Díchú insisted.

"I want to give you my barn," he said. "Obviously you can't take it with you, but you'll have it to come back to." He grinned as he added, "I know there are going to be a lot more Christians around here. It will be useful to have somewhere to gather out of the rain."

As clouds the colour of bruising rolled in from the west, Patrick had to admit that this was good thinking.

"Then I accept gratefully," he said. "It will be our first church in Ireland."

And making the sign of the Cross over Díchú and his barn, Patrick once more took to the road.

12

Míleac

⊗

The last time Patrick had crossed Ireland on foot he had been a runaway slave. He had vivid memories of being nervous and choosing the loneliest paths, shunning habitation until he was many miles from the Wood of Foclath. Now it was different. Although he knew that being a bishop was no guarantee of safety in a pagan land, he felt that he had God's authority. Instead of avoiding villages he made eagerly for every one he saw.

Sometimes, inevitably, he and his companions were seen off with stones and curses, and had to beat an undignified retreat into the trees. More often they were welcomed and given hospitality. Patrick had an attractive personality and many people were won over to the faith he preached. Some even insisted on leaving home and tagging along after him. By the time he approached the Wood of Foclath, his group of four had become a gaggle of thirty. Patrick intended to do something about this, but first there was Míleac to attend to.

Patrick had been dreaming of this meeting for years. He had imagined himself marching up to Míleac's gate, knocking with his staff and saying grandly to the gatekeeper, "I am Bishop Patrick. I have business with your master. Kindly take me to him."

The scene then shifted to Míleac's great hall. As Patrick entered, Míleac rose from his chair with a violent start of recognition. Patrick had visualised with relish the astonishment on Míleac's bearded face as he saw the gold coins glittering on the palm of his former slave. In this pleasing scenario he then invited Patrick to dinner, and the evening ended with Míleac's conversion to Christianity. What really happened was horribly different.

Míleac was a great chieftain who had many spies in the country round about. News of Patrick's coming, and the reason for it, spread rapidly. Like all such stories, this one became distorted as each teller added a few dramatic details of his own. By the time it reached Míleac's ears there was little of the truth left.

"Your runaway slave has returned with an army," gasped Míleac's informant with popping eyes. "He is a powerful servant of the new god, and he wants revenge. He intends to force you to disown your gods and worship his."

Míleac was aghast. Although he was a brave man, he was now old, and he reckoned that in a fight with Patrick he would certainly be defeated. How terrible it would be to be compelled to go on his knees to the god of his one-time slave! Míleac was a druid, and had served the old pagan gods all his life. He was determined to serve them to the end. Despairingly he piled his most treasured possessions into the middle of the great hall. When he had barricaded himself in, he began grimly to stoke the fire.

In the dusk of a winter afternoon, Patrick left his unthreatening little army to make camp beside a stream. Clutching his gold coins tightly, he came alone to the brow of a hill overlooking the valley of his captivity. It was an emotional moment. There were tears in his eyes as he looked down on Míleac's wooden farmstead, its thatched roof pink under the sinking sun. Patrick had prepared a speech, not the imperious one he had sometimes imagined, but one that was gentle and forgiving.

"Master, I come in peace . . ."

For a moment, Patrick thought it was only the fire in the great hall that was sending a dense plume of black smoke billowing into the air. But then there were flames, pink and orange tongues licking eagerly at the thatch before exploding like vast scarlet trees against the sky. Patrick stared in horror, but he knew that already Míleac was beyond help. Weeping, he turned and stumbled away. Odhrán came to meet him along the path.

"But why?" sobbed Patrick. "Why do such a terrible thing? I only wanted to meet him and put things right between us." Odhrán, who had heard the rumours, tried to explain. At first Patrick didn't understand, but as the truth dawned an impotent rage overwhelmed him. "Could Míleac really prefer such a death to believing and serving eternal God?" he asked bitterly.

"Yes," replied Odhrán, who knew Ireland and understood Míleac better than Patrick could. "For an

Irish chieftain, it was the only honourable thing to do."

If he had been alone, Patrick would have left the Wood of Foclath that very night. The place was abominable to him now. But for the first time he was responsible for others and he could see how weary his followers were. So he let them eat and sleep while he huddled in his cloak, trying desperately to make sense of what had happened. He begged God to help him, but as the wind whispered in the dark branches and the invisible stream chattered among its stones, it was the old pagan gods of Míleac who seemed to reply.

"Do not underestimate us," they said ominously, "or think that we can be conquered without sacrifice and pain. Ours is a deep magic and we have power over the minds of humankind."

In the grey light of dawn, Patrick took Auxilius and Iserninus aside.

"Listen," he said. "I've decided it's time for us to split up. You will each take ten of our converts and head east and north. Your task is to care for any people you meet who are already Christian and to carry the Gospel to those who are not. I'll take Odhrán and the remainder with me. We'll meet up at Díchú's barn at midsummer. All right?"

"Where are you going, Bishop Patrick?" asked Iserninus, both pleased and scared by the responsibility Patrick was giving him.

Patrick laughed shortly.

"I'm going south," he said. "This year I intend to celebrate Easter at Tara of the Kings."

13

Patrick's Household

&

"Why do you suppose he goes off by himself so often?" asked Brógán wistfully as he watched Patrick toiling up the windswept hill above the campsite. "Is he worried about something?"

Odhrán, who was cooking trout on hot stones over a smoky wood fire, sat back on his haunches and rubbed his stinging eyes.

"He's a bishop," he pointed out. "Of course he has things on his mind that he can't easily share with us." Then as Brógán still looked downcast he added kindly, "Listen. Why don't you tether the pony, then call the others to dinner? Caomhán and Fortcharn are mending the cart, and the rest are down by the river bathing their blisters."

He grinned encouragingly and Brógán grinned back. Still, as he strode off through the wet heather to the grassy patch where the pony was grazing, the young man couldn't help feeling depressed. When he had left home in November, love for Patrick and joy at his message had leapt in his heart. As he trekked in

Patrick's wake across Ireland, learning God's songs in the company of his fellow-converts, he had never felt tired or cold. The glow of Patrick's enthusiasm had warmed them all.

After the tragedy at the Wood of Foclath, however, the atmosphere had changed. Brógán had been thrilled to be one of the small group Patrick had chosen to accompany him, proud when Patrick humorously referred to them as his "household". The fact that there was no house didn't matter to any of them as long as they were with Patrick.

Sadly, since Míleac's suicide, Patrick hadn't been the same. His preaching still drew crowds and won converts, and to his household he was always just and kind. But the fun seemed to have drained out of him. As the little band trudged south in the February sleet behind the cart which Patrick had acquired because he had rheumatism in his knees, there were fewer songs and less laughter.

Whenever camp was made, Patrick went off on his own into a wood or up on to a lonely hillside. If he were talking to God, Brógán mused as he slipped a rope halter over the pony's grey head, God's replies didn't seem to be cheering him up much. The lines between Patrick's eyebrows had deepened into a constant frown and his curving lips were stretched into an unsmiling line.

I do hope he comes back to dinner, thought Brógán anxiously, scanning the misty hill as he led the pony home. He must be just as hungry as the rest of us. But Patrick didn't come back to dinner. Long after his household had eaten their trout and fallen asleep beside the embers of the fire, he was alone on the damp, dark hill. Míleac's death was a horror he couldn't forget, and for the first time since he had first encountered God on starry nights above the Wood of Foclath, he felt haunted by the power of evil.

It wasn't that Patrick doubted God's power, or the power that God had given him. He remembered his mother's story of how, as a small boy, he had healed his sister and how, at the worst moment of his journey with the sailors and their wolfhounds God had answered his prayer for food. Even if these things had never happened, he had seen unforgettable visions and had heard the voice of God. He had returned to Ireland full of happiness and the desire to spread the message of God's love.

Sitting in the dark on the hillside, Patrick could scarcely believe his own naivety. He had regarded the druids as tricksters, and hated the way they controlled people by making them terrified of their gods. But now he realised that he had underestimated them. It had taken Míleac's death to bring home to Patrick how strongly the druids themselves believed in the fearsome gods they worshipped. He intended to confront them in their stronghold at Tara, in the presence of High King Laoire, and he believed he would win. But for the first time he was calculating the cost of such a showdown. It was almost inevitable that more people would die, and Patrick was uneasily aware that he might have to use his own power in ways that could be misinterpreted. The last thing he wanted was to give the impression that he was a magician too. It was no wonder that the fun had drained out of Patrick, leaving him haggard and sad.

Day was breaking bleakly when he came down from the hill to find Odhrán sharing out scraps of last night's fish and some hard barley cake given to them the previous day by a friendly old woman. The little group of disconsolate, shivering figures made Patrick's heart ache, especially when he saw their anxiety on his behalf.

"Come and have some breakfast, Father."

"You're all wet. Borrow my blanket."

"Father, why don't you try to sleep in the back of the cart?"

I must pull myself together, thought Patrick guiltily. Instead of worrying about what will happen at Tara, I should be looking after these people now.

"I'm fine," he told them as he accepted his share of the food from Odhrán. "Look at the sunrise. Perhaps something good will happen today."

The first good thing that happened was that the weather improved, and spirits rose accordingly. The sun shone from a cool, early spring sky and the trees were faintly fuzzy with green. The stiff winter moorland seemed to breathe again and curlews fluted overhead. As the little procession made its way among the hills there was some tentative singing, which swelled happily when it was noticed that Patrick was joining in.

"We praise thee, O God:
We acknowledge thee to be the Lord.
All the earth doth worship thee,
The Father everlasting."

As the sun reddened and began its decline Mochonnóg, who had run ahead, came sprinting back to say that they were approaching a village. Odhrán drove the cart round a bend and Patrick saw a cluster of turf-roofed huts on the bank of a muddy brown river. There was nothing unusual in the scene, nothing to warn him that something far better than a weather-change was about to occur.

Barefoot, grubby children were first on the scene. Sucking their thumbs, they stared with round eyes as Patrick descended rather stiffly from the cart. Behind them came a slightly older boy, fair-haired and somewhat better dressed. He came forward confidently and patted the pony's head.

"What's your name, lad?" asked Patrick, eyeing him with interest.

"Beannán," was the reply. "Will you stay at my father's house tonight?"

"If he'll have me," said Patrick.

"He will," nodded Beannán.

The villagers were friendly and pleased by the excitement of having guests. All Patrick's friends were given food and shelter for the night. Patrick was entertained by Beannán's father, Conn. Conn was the village elder and his house was rather more spacious than the rest – fortunately since he had a large family. After supper Conn's wife and the younger children went off to bed in the straw at one end of the single room. Conn and Patrick sat for many hours by the fire with Beannán hovering nearby. Patrick addressed himself to Conn, telling him eagerly about his god and the peace he offered to those who served him. But all the time he was aware of the boy, shining with interest and expectation in the background.

"We'll be baptised tomorrow, won't we, Father?" Beannán burst out eventually, his eyes bright in the firelight.

Conn nodded.

"I and my house," he said gruffly to Patrick.

When he came out of Conn's house in the morning, Patrick found a sizeable group of villagers waiting shyly on the riverbank. For the first time in many days Patrick felt happy, because he realised that his household had been spreading the Gospel in the huts where they had been quartered. Brógán stood with an elderly couple and their middle-aged son. Tasach was with a young family. Mochta accompanied a woman with a baby in her arms.

Seachnall, whom Patrick had marked out as a future priest, had brought a cup of water from the river. Solemnly he held it while Patrick blessed the new converts and baptised them "in the name of the Father, the Son and the Holy Spirit". Beannán came last, his childish face rosy with delight. I wish I had a son like Beannán, thought Patrick involuntarily – and immediately felt ashamed. He was a priest. God had given him other gifts.

It was then that something wonderful happened. Patrick had thanked Conn for his hospitality and said goodbye, promising to visit again later in the year. He had one foot on the cart and the other still on the ground when Beannán darted out from the doorway. Grabbing Patrick's leg with both hands he cried, "Please, let me go with Patrick, my true father. I know

God wants me to be with him!"

It was a very tense moment. Gently Patrick disengaged the clinging hands and turned to look at Conn. He had a vivid recollection of his own father's face on the morning when he left Bannavem Taberniae for the last time. His heart went out to Conn.

"Beannán is only a child," Patrick said. "Obviously I can't take him with me unless you approve."

There was a long, painful pause before Conn said, "I have other sons. I shall give Beannán to God and to you, Patrick. Take good care of him."

Patrick nodded with a smile.

"Lift Beannán onto the cart," he instructed Fortcharn, who was standing by the pony's head. "He is the heir to my kingdom."

"Goodbye," Beannán called. "Thank you, Father!"

Odhrán shook the reins. The cart jolted and trundled out onto the open moor. Patrick looked sidelong at the new member of his household, sitting perkily between himself and Odhrán. Oh dear, thought Patrick. I don't know anything about children, and I'm old enough to be this boy's grandfather. But somehow he knew that everything would work out well.

14

High King Laoire

As winter finally loosened its grip and the leaves thickened, each day brought Patrick and his household closer to the High King's fortress at Tara. Beannán diverted everyone, playing hide and seek with Brógán and Tasach, going fishing with Odhrán, chasing rabbits and imitating birdsong. Patrick watched him with pride, already planning his education and dreaming of the day when Beannán would succeed him as a bishop in Ireland.

It was a welcome distraction from his anxiety about the coming tussle at Tara. The thought of matching the druids trick for trick became ever more dreadful to Patrick, yet he couldn't see what else was to be done. He could only hope that when the time came God would guide him to take the right decisions.

On the Thursday before Easter Patrick and his companions made their way along the Boyne river towards the green hill of Slane.

"Do you want to make for Tara?" asked Odhrán, who as usual was driving the cart. He looked across the wide plain of Maigh Bhreagha and added, "We could be there early tomorrow."

Patrick shook his head.

"No," he said. "I've decided to camp on the hill of Slane and celebrate Easter there. Then perhaps I'll go to visit the druids – or perhaps they'll come to visit me."

"Just as you say," agreed Odhrán, turning the pony's head in the direction of the hill.

Meanwhile, unknown to Patrick, the High King Laoire was also an anxious man. In his wood and wattle hall at Tara, he sometimes felt little better than a prisoner. Ever since he had succeeded his famous father Niall Naoighiallach as High King, he had been surrounded by uppity, self-important druids. Night and day they told him what to do and warned him what the future might bring. Laoire didn't much like these shrill-voiced soothsayers who flapped about the palace like vast yellow birds, yet he dared not send them packing. He believed in the old gods and feared their displeasure more than anything.

As the great spring festival approached when lesser kings, princes, druids and magicians were due to gather at Tara, High King Laoire was even more fidgety than usual. His own druids had been alarming him with prophecies of a new way of life which would come from across the sea. The kings of Ireland would then depart, they foretold gloomily, and the gods would be destroyed. The chief druid Lúchath Maol had recited to Laoire a verse which the High King found incomprehensible and threatening at the same time.

High King Laoire

"Shaven-head will come
With his crooked stick
And his house with a hole in its head.
He will chant blasphemy from his table
At the front of his house.
All his household will answer,
'Let it be so, let it be so.'
When all this happens
Our pagan rule will be over at last."

"What on earth does it mean?" demanded Laoire impatiently.

The chief druid waggled his beard.

"It is a warning," he said importantly. "When the shaven-headed one comes, we must be ready to resist him with all our power."

Laoire shivered and drew his stool closer to the fire. News of the strife and turmoil engulfing Europe had reached Ireland, and the notion of a bald barbarian from the east invading and laying siege to Tara didn't seem far-fetched. The next time the druids annoyed him with their pushiness the High King stifled his feelings. Suddenly they seemed his only bulwark against disaster.

While he sat brooding, preparations for a great feast to welcome Laoire's guests went on in the palace kitchen. Oxen and pigs were roasted. Loaves were baked. Game hung from the rafters in the smoke. Out of doors wood was collected for a huge fire in honour of the gods. It was the custom that on the most magical night of the year, no fire in Ireland was lit before that of the High King.

15

A Contest by Night

⊗

Good Friday passed quietly. Fortcharn and Tasach, the handymen of Patrick's household, set up a canopy of animal skins on four straight branches. They built a little altar of wood where Patrick celebrated Mass and read from the Gospels. From his hillside camp he could see, down on the plain, processions of gleaming chariots converging on Tara. Obviously some great pagan gathering was taking place. Good, thought Patrick grimly. If God and I are going to have a showdown with the High King and the druids, the more people who witness our victory the better. Yet still he dreaded what was to come.

On Saturday, Patrick sent his companions down into a forest to collect wood.

"I'm going to light a fire this evening," he told them, "to remind us of Christ's light entering the world on Easter Day."

Patrick didn't know – and wouldn't have cared if he had – the rule that on that night the High King's fire must be lit before any other. In the still twilight he lit his and watched it burn, fierce as the sun, clear as the moon.

Down on the plain of Maigh Bhreagha, villagers peeped in awe from their doors at the great light shining from the hill of Slane.

"Who can have dared to disobey the order of the High King?" they whispered, before creeping away fearfully to their straw beds.

At Tara, where the blaze of Patrick's fire was clearly seen across the flat countryside, the reaction was noisier.

"Who has dared to commit such a crime in my kingdom?" roared High King Laoire when the news was brought to him by white-faced guards. "He must die!"

The courtiers and guests assembling for supper in the great hall looked nervously at Laoire. His huge body was shaking and his red-bearded face was lurid in the smoky torchlight.

"I don't know," said someone loudly, starting a babble of denial.

"Don't ask me."

"I haven't a clue."

"Must be someone mad, surely."

Then the druids arrived. The company parted respectfully as they sailed in procession up the hall. They surrounded the dais where Laoire sat with his Queen, their yellow robes billowing. Lúchath Maol was their spokesman.

"Eternal life to you, O King," he snapped, then got down to business. Rolling his eyes till the whites showed, he began to sway to and fro. "The fire lit before the one in your house," he droned, "will never be put out unless it is put out tonight. If it burns until morning, the man who lit it and the kingdom he brings will rule over us for ever."

"Then what are we waiting for?" yelled Laoire, jumping up and almost knocking Lúchath Maol over. "We must go at once, extinguish the fire and kill the one who threatens us."

Supper was forgotten as an excited rabble poured out of the hall into the cold evening air. Soon the High King's chariot was thundering through the gate of Tara, followed by twenty-six others carrying warlike princes and chanting druids. Lúchath Maol and his assistant Lochra travelled just behind the High King and his Queen. Under the stars the procession lurched across the plain. The drumbeat of many hoofs was audible to Patrick and his friends long before they saw the ominous shapes of horses and chariots under the rising moon.

"This is it, then," said Odhrán, his bearded face intense in the firelight.

Patrick nodded.

"Beannán," he said, "stay with Odhrán and whatever happens, don't be afraid."

"I'm not afraid," burst out Beannán indignantly.

"I am," admitted Brógán in a small voice.

Quietly the household formed a line behind the canopy. Patrick sat under it with the altar behind him and the fire on his right. He waited impassively as the High King and his attendants dismounted and began to move on foot towards him. Laoire came first, a burly, hairy man with a gold circlet round his low forehead. Just behind him walked four druids. Patrick saw them pause and confer in whispers just outside the circle of firelight. The High King then sat down on a convenient tree stump and the druids ran round telling everyone else to sit down too.

"What's going on?" demanded Beannán in a high voice, but Patrick said, "Sh-sh!" With dignity he rose and advanced towards the High King, repeating the words of a psalm. *"Some trust in chariots and some in horses, but we will remember the name of the Lord our God."*

Afterwards he would be puzzled by a look of horrified recognition which he saw in the High King's eyes. At the time he was diverted by an incident which was gratifying to him, though embarrassing to Laoire. Obviously the druids had advised the High King to stay outside the circle of light cast by the holy fire, and told everyone to stay seated as a snub to Patrick. As Patrick approached, however, one of the druids, Earc by name, rose and bowed to him.

"God bless you, my son," said Patrick, looking steadily into the surprised young face. "Go and join my household."

Earc hesitated only for an instant. He looked fearfully at the High King, and at Lúchath Maol's furious face. Then he kirtled up his yellow robes and bounded across the grass to Patrick's friends.

Next to step forward was Lochra, a druid second only to Lúchath Maol in magical prowess. He fixed Patrick with a malevolent eye.

"You are a rogue," he said coldly. "You dishonour the true gods with your unlawful fire. May your false god be cursed and you with him, evil one."

It was a dreadful moment. The insult to himself didn't matter to Patrick, but the insult to God scandalised him. He wanted to strike Lochra down where he stood. Just in time he remembered that only God had the right to decide the time of someone's death – and even as the warning crossed his mind God did just that. In an instant a wild wind whirled out of the motionless trees, snatching angrily at Lochra's robes. Patrick saw the druid's mouth gaping in terror as he was drawn in an upward spiral to the level of the treetops.

"Lord, you have everything in your power," whispered Patrick as the shriek of the wind suddenly cut out and Lochra fell. The druid's head hit a rock with a sickening smack. A shudder of fear ran through the pagan throng.

"Seize that man who is trying to destroy us," screamed Laoire.

"May the Lord come and scatter his enemies," retorted Patrick.

No sooner had he spoken than thick clouds whipped across the moon. Patrick's fire died to a ghostly flicker, although it did not go out. In the darkness the pagans panicked and ran. Those who made it to their chariots whipped up their terrified horses and fled, trampling others remorselessly under flying hoofs. The earth shook and Patrick's companions fell to their knees, trembling and calling for mercy.

Then, just as suddenly, all was quiet again. The moon reappeared and the fire blazed up. In its light

A Contest by Night

Patrick saw Laoire's Queen, a pale, dark-haired woman in a green dress, walking over the churned-up grass towards him. Considering what she had just witnessed, she was remarkably calm. When she addressed him her words were polite and conciliatory, but there was a shifty look in her black eyes which put Patrick on his guard.

"Just and powerful man," said the Queen, "please do not destroy the King. He has seen enough to convince him, and he is willing to worship your god."

"Let him come forward," Patrick replied.

The Queen turned and beckoned. Laoire emerged, pale and dishevelled, from the shadows beyond the ring of fire. With downcast eyes he knelt before Patrick and asked in a whining voice for his blessing.

But Patrick wasn't a fool. He knew that Laoire only wanted to buy time, and he decided to do the same. There had been enough drama for one night.

"There are dead and wounded among your followers," Patrick said. "Go and see to them now. Tomorrow I shall come to visit you. If you are in earnest, I shall gladly bless you then."

16

Tara of the Kings

When the High King and the last of his followers had departed, the mood among Patrick's followers was gleeful. Their grinning faces angered Patrick and for once he rebuked them.

"This is no time for rejoicing," he told them sternly. "People have died here tonight, one of them in a way that should scare you stiff. This isn't a game. Stop behaving so childishly and go to sleep. There will be more danger to face tomorrow."

Silent and subdued, the household fetched cloaks and blankets and lay down for the night. Patrick sat close to his fire, staring out across the plain at the twinkling lights of Tara. He was sure that God had intervened that night to save him from the sin of killing another human being and it was a relief to feel that God was sanctioning unusual methods to defeat the champions of the old gods. But Patrick knew that tomorrow would be different. Tomorrow he must establish his own authority. God would empower him, but wouldn't take decisions out of his hands. Dawn was breaking and the Easter fire was almost out when Patrick too wrapped himself in his cloak and lay down to snatch a couple of hours of sleep.

It was fifteen miles across country to Tara, and Patrick was determined to set off early.

"We'll all walk," he told Odhrán, adding with a wry smile, "I don't fancy arriving at the High King's court riding behind a skinny pony on a battered old cart."

So, leaving the former druid Earc to look after the camp, the little procession set out. Patrick and Beannán walked in front while Odhrán brought up the rear.

"Fancy me going to the High King's house," said Beannán wonderingly. "This is exciting, isn't it, Father?"

"Very," agreed Patrick dryly.

Apparently they were expected at Tara. As Patrick approached the gates were flung open, and they passed so quickly through the courtyard and outer hall that they had the impression of walking through closed doors. In the smoky, windowless great hall High King Laoire and his friends were at dinner. Silence fell as Patrick entered, and in the wavering orange torchlight hundreds of eyes stared at him. Hostility was palpable, but also fear. Last night's events had made a deep impression on everyone.

Once again, however, Patrick was heartened by an unexpected defection from Laoire's ranks. While everyone else remained seated, a man called Dubhthach mac Lughair rose and saluted Patrick. Dubhthach was a poet, an honoured bard of the High King, and his changing sides infuriated Laoire. Still, remembering that he was now posing as a Christian himself, the High King forced a smile as Patrick blessed Dubhthach and invited him to join his company.

"Come and eat with us, Patrick," invited Laoire smoothly, and a space was made for Patrick between him and Lúchath Maol. "Some wine for our guest," he added, and immediately a servant stepped forward with a silver cup.

Patrick sat down and presently Lúchath Maol made the first move. While Patrick had his head turned towards the High King, the druid took a small phial from the folds of his robe. He tipped one drop of bright green liquid into Patrick's wine.

Patrick knew perfectly well what had been done, and that everyone was watching – hoping, probably, that he would be poisoned. He intended to disappoint them. Lifting the cup he blessed it and the wine instantly froze like ice. Standing so that all could see, Patrick turned the cup upside down. There was a gasp of amazement as the green globule fell like an emerald and shattered on the table. Patrick sat down and blessed the cup again. When the wine returned to normal he took a sip of it.

Lúchath Maol was impressed, but reckoned that he had some even better tricks up his sleeve. Just as the meal was ending he said loudly to Patrick, "Let's go and work some wonders out of doors."

Patrick wasn't keen, but everybody else was. Led by the High King and Queen the company rose and poured excitedly out of the palace on to the green sward before the gates. Chairs were brought for the royal couple, while the rest jostled like any crowd of spectators for the best positions.

"Well, what do you suggest?" Patrick enquired.

"Let's make snow over the whole plain," replied Lúchath Maol.

"It is God who should control the weather," Patrick pointed out, but the druid paid no attention. Under the eager eyes of the crowd he began to sway, stamping and reciting spells. Lúchath Maol was a master of illusion and mass hypnosis, a mere magician but a clever one. He had no difficulty in persuading the credulous onlookers that they were seeing the plain of Maigh Bhreagha under a mantle of snow. Patrick shrugged his shoulders. "Now why don't you remove it?" he said.

Patrick's unimpressed tone needled Lúchath Maol and forced him into making a mistake.

"I can't, until this time tomorrow," he said tartly.

"Well, I can," Patrick replied.

He held up his hand and made the sign of the Cross. His mind-power was even stronger than Lúchath Maol's and in an instant the plain appeared green again.

"Fog, then," snapped the druid and the whole performance had to be gone through again.

It was the longest, weariest day Patrick had ever spent. Angrier and more frustrated by the minute, Lúchath Maol produced every trick in his repertoire, tricks with water, tricks with fire. On every occasion Patrick outsmarted him. By evening even the High King had had enough. Irritably he ordered that the contest should stop, but couldn't conceal his anger and disappointment. Discarding his pretence of conversion, he blurted out bitterly what he was really thinking.

"I have a good mind to kill you," he growled at Patrick, showing his yellow teeth. "I knew when I saw you last night who you were, the shaven-headed one who threatens to destroy me and our ancient way of life."

Patrick was tired. He looked into Laoire's furious, bulbous eyes and decided that he'd had enough.

"Listen to me," he said icily. "Last night you tried to deceive me and my god. Now is your last chance. If you don't repent and believe now, you'll die on the spot. Frankly, you deserve to have the wrath of heaven on your head."

There was a terrible pause. Laoire narrowed his eyes, trying to read in Patrick's face a sign that he was bluffing. Gradually he took in the fact that Patrick was in earnest. The High King shivered visibly.

"I need time to consult my council," he muttered, getting up from his chair.

"Don't keep me waiting long," warned Patrick grimly. "Your time is running out."

Laoire withdrew indoors with as much dignity as he could muster. His followers, their party mood snuffed out, went warily after him. Patrick and his household were left alone in the chilly courtyard.

"You were wonderful, Father," ventured Brógán.

"Yes, you were wonderful," echoed Beannán, almost asleep on his feet. "Father, can we go back to our camp soon?"

"Very soon," Patrick promised.

Indeed, they did not have long to wait. A servant came and respectfully summoned Patrick to the High King. Laoire rose from his throne as Patrick entered the hall. With the members of his council he went down on his knees. They didn't look a joyful group of converts, but Patrick was satisfied with what the High King said.

"It is better for me to believe than to die. I am ready to become a Christian, and of course my household will do as I do."

"Very well. This time you must keep your word," Patrick replied.

17

Droim Saileach

⊗

Patrick knew better than to suppose that the reluctant
conversion of the High King would make Ireland
Christian overnight. But it was very important. In
those days, when a king or even the head of an
ordinary household converted, everyone in his
jurisdiction did too. Many of those converted with
Laoire became more enthusiastic Christians than he
was. Over a period of years power swung away from
the druids to the Christian church.

Glad to have the abnormal events at Tara behind
him, Patrick went on travelling all over Ireland. He
went south of the Shannon and away to the lonely
loughs and glens of the west. Everywhere he preached
the Gospel and founded churches, convents and
monasteries. It delighted him that so many of his
converts wanted to devote their lives entirely to God.

The life Patrick led was hard for a man no longer
young, but with the success of his mission serenity
returned to him. He was used to sleeping under the
stars in wild, lonely places and took in his stride

ambushes and even occasional beatings by bandits.

The original household changed. Seachnall, Mochta and the former druid Earc went to Britain to study for the priesthood. Dubhthach joined for a while and Mochonnóg left to become a monk. Others came and went. Only Odhrán, whom Patrick laughingly called "my charioteer", Brógán and Beannán were always there.

Patrick watched over Beannán with anxious pride, but as the boy grew up he gave his adopted father no cause for anxiety. Beannán had a still, shining quality which impressed everyone who met him, and Patrick had already discussed with him the possibility that God might wish him to become Bishop of Ireland one day.

"When you are eighteen," Patrick said, "I shall send you to train as a priest. When you come back, perhaps I'll be able to retire."

Beannán burst out laughing.

"I don't think you'd like that at all, Father," he said.

Patrick didn't really think he would either. All the same, as he got older and stiffer in the mornings, he couldn't help wishing that he at least had somewhere he could call home. Somewhere to come back to after long journeys and have an occasional rest. A watertight cell would be nice, with a church nearby and perhaps a garden. He would grow apple trees and watch the bean pods swelling in the sun.

For a long time this remained a dream with which Patrick sometimes beguiled himself on cold, wet nights. It wasn't until he began to think that he needed headquarters, other than Díchú's barn, for his work that it occurred to him that this might also be a place specially his own.

Like many busy people, Patrick turned his idea over in his head for a long time without acting on it. He had passed Ard Mhacha several times before it occurred to him that the hill there might be just the place he needed. One summer he had paid a visit to the convent of Bríd in Kildare and on a golden August afternoon was travelling north to a meeting with Auxilius and Iserninus at Díchú's barn. Once again he saw the hilltop rising like a green tonsure from a fringe of willow leaves.

"That would be a wonderful place for a church," he remarked to Beannán, who was walking beside the cart. *"A city that is set on a hill cannot be hid."*

"I'm sure you can have it if you want it," said Beannán, who knew of Patrick's desire for a centre for his mission. "All the land round here belongs to Dáire of Airthir, and he's sympathetic to our work. Why don't you go and ask him?"

"Good idea," said Patrick, making up his mind on the spur of the moment. "Make for Dáire's farm, Odhrán. Maybe he'll ask us to supper and give us beds for the night."

Dáire did ask them to supper and said that they were welcome to sleep in his barn. After a splendid meal of salmon, barley cake, curd cheese and blackberries Patrick explained to Dáire how much he needed a piece of land for a new church.

"I'm hoping you'll be able to help," he said frankly.

Dáire was a strange mix of a man – wealthy, proud, touchy, quick-tempered and generous when he was in the mood. He also knew the value of what belonged to him.

"Which piece of land had you in mind?" he asked, and scratched his fair beard when he heard the answer. "Droim Saileach? The hilltop at Ard Mhacha?" he repeated, then pursed his lips. "I'd have to think about that."

"I'd be so grateful," said Patrick. "It seems the perfect place for a church and monastery and – I must admit – a cell for me. I can't afford to pay you. Every penny I've ever had I've given to the sick and needy. But you would have God's blessing, which is worth more than gold."

Dáire raised his eyebrows. Like many rich people he had his doubts about this. He knew he was being wheedled and felt some irritation. On the other hand, he knew how Patrick had discredited the druids at Tara, and didn't want to offend someone so obviously powerful. After some thought he tried to compromise.

"I'll tell you what," he said. "I'm not keen to part with the hilltop, but I'll give you a site further down. You'll have room for the buildings you mention and fields for grazing and growing crops. How will that do?"

Patrick was disappointed, but he knew that it was a fair offer. He must make the best of it.

"Thank you, Dáire," he said. "That will do very well indeed."

The following morning Patrick despatched Odhrán and Brógán with a message to Auxilius and Iserninus at Díchú's barn.

"Tell them to come and meet me here," he said, "and bring our other friends too. We'll need plenty of hands to help with the building."

Brógán and Odhrán went off in the cart while Patrick and Beannán passed the time by making a few visits in the district. By the middle of September building materials were assembled and workers ready to begin. Even Iserninus and Auxilius, who came thinking that as assistant bishops they were really too grand to soil their hands, were infected by the general excitement. After their conference with Patrick they stayed for a few weeks to lend a hand. All through the autumn work went on; a ditch was dug and a woven fence erected around the area which Patrick had marked out for the monastery and church. Brógán planted fruit trees and Odhrán made pens for the sheep and cows which friendly neighbours had promised Patrick.

It should have been a happy time for Patrick, and he did enjoy hearing young voices singing and seeing the beginning of the city of God he had long envisaged. Yet through all the mellow, amber weeks he felt irritable and tired. It wasn't just that he felt age seeping into his bones and rheumatism gripping him cruelly on frosty mornings. He was peeved because Dáire had refused to give him Droim Saileach, the willow-ringed ridge on top of the hill.

Often Patrick climbed stiffly up through the trees to the green summit. Lowering himself on to the grass, he sat looking out across a shimmering plain to the mauve mountains draped on the horizon. This is the place I want, he grumbled to himself. It was mean of Dáire not to let me have it. Perhaps it wasn't surprising that one small, annoying incident ignited Patrick's smouldering discontent. It led to the most absurd happenings of his whole ministry in Ireland.

18

Dáire and the Lazy Horse

⚘

The trouble began with a horse. Towards dusk one evening Patrick looked out from the gate and saw Eoghan, Dáire's stableman, leading an old and stubborn-looking mare into a meadow which, by agreement, was now Patrick's. Patrick watched in astonishment as Eoghan turned the horse loose and the creature began to crop the grass. Then he lost his temper.

"Oi!" bellowed Patrick, running as best he could down the slope and grabbing the man by his tunic. "What d'you think you're doing, eh? Take that brute out of my field this minute and feed him somewhere else."

Eoghan was a surly fellow at the best of times. Now it was late and he wanted his supper. Angrily he shook off Patrick's hand. He didn't say a word, but with an insolent shrug stumped off in the direction of Dáire's farm. Patrick was left practically hopping up and down with rage. It was too late to do anything more that night, but he wasn't going to leave the matter there.

I'll go and have this out with Dáire in the morning, he thought grimly as he closed the gate. It was at this point that the affair took a ridiculous turn.

Next morning, just as he was about to set off for Dáire's farm, Patrick saw Eoghan lurching out of the meadow. His face was as white as a sheet.

"My master's horse is dead," Patrick heard him bawling. "You're in trouble now, Christian!"

Patrick didn't feel threatened by these words, although he resented their tone. Stepping lightly through the dewy grass he examined the rickety animal lying stretched out in the middle of the meadow. The eyes were closed and the flanks barely moving, but a thin vapour from the nostrils formed and vanished on the frosty air. Not so much dead as bone lazy, thought Patrick, grinning as he turned back to the path.

It was a pleasant morning, and much of his good humour was restored as he strolled through the crisp October wood towards Dáire's farm.

Meanwhile, there had been a dramatic scene in the farm kitchen. According to Odhrán, who had heard the story from Dáire's wife and passed it on to Patrick later, Eoghan had blundered into the kitchen yelling, "Master! That Christian Patrick has killed your horse! He wants to punish you for pasturing an animal in his field!"

Dáire too was in a bad mood. His children had been cheeky and he had a sore toe. Leaping to his feet he shouted, "I'd like to kill that man!"

Rushing to the door he tripped, fell to the ground and knocked himself unconscious.

"Oh dear," cried his poor wife. "This is what comes of quarrelling over an old horse! Run to Patrick. Tell him what's happened and ask him to be merciful. We need his help."

Then she got down on her knees and energetically began to slap her husband's face.

By this time Patrick was halfway to the farm. What's wrong now? he wondered wearily as he saw Eoghan and another farm labourer panting towards him through the trees.

"Our master Dáire has collapsed," gasped Eoghan's companion. "He is very ill. Please, give us something to make him better."

Patrick, who knew Dáire well, had a fairly good idea of what might have happened. But he said nothing as he took the water bottle he always carried out of his belt. Making the sign of the Cross over it, he handed it to the man.

"Sprinkle some of this water on Dáire's face," he said. "He will be well again by evening."

The man ran off with the bottle, but Eoghan hesitated. He squinted at Patrick, his expression half admiring, half afraid.

"Would it – um, work on the horse?" he asked sheepishly.

Patrick looked in exasperation at the round, foolish face.

"You could try it and see," he said sarcastically, then immediately wished that he hadn't. People like Eoghan didn't understand irony.

In the afternoon, when Patrick was sitting on Droim Saileach, Odhrán climbed up and sat beside him.

"What's amusing you?" asked Patrick, suspiciously eyeing his friend's grinning face.

Odhrán could scarcely tell him for laughing.

"I had to go to Dáire's place to ask permission to cut more wattles," he said. "I didn't see him but his wife was in a great state. Apparently you didn't only raise Dáire from the dead this morning, you raised his nag as well!"

Patrick groaned.

"Do people really believe such things?" he asked, shaking his head.

"Oh yes," Odhrán assured him. "It's no wonder you're becoming famous."

19

"Grazacham"

※

Patrick went to bed that night shaking his head over human foolishness. There was more foolishness to come, however, and later he had to admit that some of it was his own.

Patrick hoped that he might now have a rest from Dáire, but it was not to be. Next morning, as he was returning to his cell from the makeshift church, he saw the farmer coming through the gate. Dáire walked straight towards Patrick, staggering under the weight of an enormous bronze bowl. Its highly polished surface gleamed in the sunlight, and Patrick couldn't help admiring its beautifully embossed sides. But he didn't covet possessions and he was taken aback when Dáire put the bowl down and said proudly, "Look! This is a present for you."

Patrick usually spoke Irish, but he had just finished saying Mass and Latin was still in his mind.

"*Gratias agam,*" he muttered, wondering what on earth he was going to do with the bowl. "I give thanks."

That was when things began to go wrong again. Patrick had lost some teeth and his diction wasn't as clear as it had once been. Dáire was slightly deaf and didn't understand a word of Latin. His face reddened as he repeated what he thought he had heard.

"Grazacham?" he spluttered indignantly. "Grazacham? What kind of word is that, I'd like to know?"

The sound of this nonsense word made Patrick burst out laughing.

"Grazacham, Dáire," he chortled. "Grazacham!"

Unfortunately Dáire wasn't in the mood for jokes. He thought Patrick was mocking him and despising his present. Before Patrick could explain he had turned on his heel and stomped angrily away.

Oh dear, Patrick sighed as he watched Dáire going huffily down the track. That was a mistake. I shouldn't have laughed. But Dáire was gone, so he picked up the bowl and took it to the monks who were preparing vegetables for the community's dinner. The monks dropped their knives, exclaiming delightedly at such a useful gift.

"I wouldn't start using it yet, if I were you," warned Patrick ruefully. "Something tells me it will be taken back before today is over."

Patrick was right. An hour or so later, as he sat reading a psalm at the door of his wattle cell, two of Dáire's servants came in at the gate. Sheepishly they approached Patrick.

"Our master is offended by the way you received his gift," said one, avoiding Patrick's eye.

"We have orders to take the bowl back," said the other, blushing in embarrassment.

Suddenly Patrick was bored with the whole business. What a fuss about a bowl, he thought irritably.

"Oh, grazacham," he snapped, pointing the men in the direction of the kitchen. "Take it away," he ordered, returning his attention to his book.

Patrick reckoned he had seen the last of the bowl, but by evening he was regretting having teased Dáire and growled at his servants. He knew that he owed Dáire debts of kindness and ought not to fall out with him. I'll walk over to Dáire's house, he decided. It's time to apologise and put things right. But before he could put on his cloak and find his walking-stick, Dáire appeared at the gate. Again he was carrying the bronze bowl.

Suddenly aware of the absurdity of the situation, the two men looked at each other with twinkling eyes and twitching lips.

"'Grazacham' when you get a present. 'Grazacham' when it's taken away," said Dáire. "You're a fine one with your 'grazachams'! But let's not fight over anything so ridiculous. The bowl is yours." And while Patrick, shamed by such generosity, was trying to find an answer, Dáire went on, "By the way – I've been thinking. There's really no good reason why you shouldn't have the ground you first asked for. Droim Saileach is yours. Take it, and welcome."

This time Patrick didn't say, "Grazacham." For a moment he was speechless with delight, then he grasped Dáire warmly by the hand.

"Oh, thank you," he said in familiar Irish. "I can't tell you how much this means to me."

Again the best of friends, Patrick and Dáire climbed the hill together. The sun was rolling like a crimson wheel on the western horizon and mist was rising thinly from the grass. Odhrán, Beannán and Brógán followed at a distance, and so witnessed something they would remember all their lives.

Near the summit of the hill, a beautiful doe was lying with a delicate fawn curled up against her warm flank. Odhrán, who had a hunter's instinct, would have chased the animals and killed them, but when he started forward Patrick imperiously waved him back. As the startled fawn rose tremulously on his frail legs, Patrick stepped lightly forward and held out his hand. Like a dog confident of his master's affection the fawn came and put his soft nose into the outstretched palm.

Dáire, Odhrán, Beannán and Brógán watched in amazement as stiff, elderly Patrick lifted the fawn across his shoulders, as easily as he had lifted lambs when he was Míleac's shepherd long ago. With the doe following him like a faithful, loving sheep Patrick carried the fawn down through the willows and across a stream to the next hill. Carefully he set the creature down and watched tenderly as mother and son leapt away on their dancers' feet into a wood.

I'll build the altar of my new church where the deer were lying, Patrick thought as he walked home in the twilight. As he thanked God, a great peace enfolded him.

20

A Dangerous Encounter

⧉

If Patrick's followers groaned inwardly when they learned that they would have to dismantle all the buildings they had erected and move them further up the hill, they were too well disciplined to let their feelings show. Patrick was like a father to them but he was also their ruler. He had trained them to obey. As soon as spring came they set to work, and by the next year's end Patrick's dream of "a city set on a hill" had come true.

It really was a holy city, devoted entirely to God. On Droim Saileach stood a wooden church roofed with turf, its altar raised over the spot where the doe and her fawn had lain. Around the church were wattle huts for the priests and monks of Patrick's now extensive household. Below the line of willows were the kitchen, dining-room and guest-house; further down still, protected by a ditch and a stout fence, stood a barn, a byre and enclosures for the animals which kind friends had given Patrick. Beyond the gate were the orchard and fields where the monks grew barley.

It was a busy, energetic community, and Patrick was happy to share work and worship with his friends. But he built his own cell apart from the rest. He chose a little promontory where he could sit on a wooden stool in the evening, gazing out over countryside tumbling like sea towards the mountains. As the stars came out he thanked God for his goodness and heard God's voice answering in the wind. *"Fear not, for I am with thee."*

Even in winter, when the monks had to break ice on the stream to get water and everyone was shivering with cold, Patrick admired the lacing of hoar frost on the willows and the runes made by birds' feet in the snow. Often he wished that he could settle down in his cell and spend the rest of his days within the sound of the sanctuary bell. But he knew that his travelling days weren't over yet. There was too much missionary work still to be done. In the spring Patrick would resignedly mount the cart and with Odhrán, Beannán, Brógán and a few other disciples set out on yet another journey.

Patrick's fear that his triumph over Lúchath Maol at Tara would give him an unwelcome reputation as a wonder-worker was well founded. People were credulous and superstitious, and Patrick sometimes stamped with frustration when he heard yet another unlikely tale about himself – that he had raised a dead horse, or that he had made his fingers light up like lamps in the dark. One day he heard that at his command all the snakes in Ireland had obligingly slithered into the sea! Such stories upset Patrick because he felt that they diminished his real, God-given power.

Only very occasionally, as at Tara, he was forced to do something spectacular because there seemed no other way of attaining a good end. This was what happened on the day when he encountered Mac Cuill mac Greacha, one of the most wicked men in Ireland.

Mac Cuill, a man so ugly that he was nicknamed "Cyclops", was the leader of a savage gang of bandits. They lived in a lonely mountain glen in the north of Ireland, preying on innocent travellers, beating and often killing them. Patrick had heard of Mac Cuill and Mac Cuill had heard of Patrick, but not until a July afternoon did the two come face to face.

Patrick had been preaching at Díchú's barn and was longing to get back to his cell at Ard Mhacha. When the axle of the cart broke he rather impatiently left Odhrán to mend it, setting off on foot with Brógán and Beannán.

"We'll take a short cut through the mountains," he told Odhrán. "Follow on as soon as you can."

Life with Patrick had taught Beannán to take some danger in his stride. He'd been in sinister places before. Yet as the trio left the sunny uplands and entered a dark cleft between two cliff-faces, Beannán felt fear trickling coldly down his spine.

"I don't like this place, Father," he confided nervously, raising his eyes to a hawk hovering ominously above the chasm. He had a horrible feeling that he might be its prey.

Brógán too shivered as the sides of the glen suddenly shut out the sun.

"You're right, Beannán," he whispered. "I think there are eyes watching us."

"God's eyes are watching us," said Patrick firmly. "Don't be afraid, my sons."

Brógán was speaking the truth, however. Other eyes than God's were watching them. They were the eyes of Mac Cuill. High on a wooded ledge the brigand watched eagerly the three figures filing along beside a black mountain stream. Mac Cuill had spies everywhere and he knew who the old man was. His close-set eyes gleamed with bitter satisfaction that an opportunity long dreamt of had come at last. He raised his sunburnt hand and at once his followers came pouncing out from behind the rocks. Silently they surrounded Mac Cuill. Their eyes lit up too when he pointed out the travellers far below.

"Easy pickings," gloated one.

"Shall we go?" laughed another.

But Mac Cuill said, "No. That's Patrick, the conjuror who deceives people by doing tricks in the name of some foreign god. We'll get no loot from him, boys, but I aim to have some fun with him. Give him the opportunity to do one more trick before I finish him off."

Mac Cuill would have found it hard to say why Patrick's reputation outraged him so much. Desperation had made him wicked and he had long ago stopped believing in any god at all, yet he had always had a troubled conscience. Somehow the wild tales he had heard about Patrick's wonder-working disgusted him. He would have been amazed to learn that Patrick's attitude to these exaggerated claims was exactly the same as his own.

"We'll climb along the cliff and drop down at the

end of the glen," said Mac Cuill. "Earnán, you will lie down and pretend to be ill. We'll ask the conjuror to cast some spells and see if he can cure you. When he can't –"

Mac Cuill broke off, drawing his finger meaningfully across his throat. Everyone laughed. The bandits began to creep on agile feet along the cliff. Mac Cuill paused to whet his knife.

Meanwhile, Patrick, Brógán and Beannán were getting along as well as they could over the loose, sharp stones. Patrick sensed the terror of his young companions and felt sorry for them.

"As soon as we're through the glen we'll look for somewhere to spend the night," he said encouragingly, although he was the sorest and most exhausted of the three.

He was also the least alarmed when, near the mouth of the glen, they found their way blocked by a huddle of dirty, tough-looking men. They were grouped around a body that lay shivering and groaning under a grubby blanket. Patrick knew that this was Mac Cuill's country and it had crossed his mind that the bandit might set a trap for him. He heard Brógán utter a sharp squawk of fear.

"Listen," said Patrick urgently. "You must both keep quiet and leave this to me. Whatever happens, don't show surprise. Understand?"

Beannán and Brógán nodded, whey-faced. As they cowered behind Patrick, one of the bandits left the group and came running towards them.

"Look," cried the man, feigning alarm. "One of our company has just become ill. Come and say some of your spells over him!" The word "spells" made Patrick's jaw stiffen, but he moved towards Mac Cuill and his gang without comment. Beannán and Brógán scurried at his heels, not wanting to be separated from him. "Perhaps you can make him recover," added the messenger with a leer.

Patrick looked gravely at the figure writhing and moaning under the blanket. He was aware of vindictive looks but gave no sign of concern.

"I could certainly cure him," he said. "That is –" There was a rustle of gleeful expectation. "That is, if he were really ill."

The sigh of disappointment from the onlookers was as audible as the wind in the leaves. Mac Cuill spat into the stream and ostentatiously fingered his knife.

"You may as well get up, Earnán," he said.

Then events took an unexpected turn.

With a final jerk, the man on the ground stopped moving. But he didn't get up and a long, nervous moment passed before one of the gang stepped forward and tweaked the blanket away. In total silence everyone looked at Earnán's milk-white face with its round, open mouth and unnaturally staring eyes. His thin body was as rigid as a spear.

A hoarse voice said, "He's dead." Brógán and Beannán looked at each other in bewilderment. Could Patrick, of all people, actually have killed someone? In despair they gave themselves up for lost.

The reaction of Mac Cuill and his men, however, wasn't what the two young men expected. Instead of roaring with rage and whipping out their weapons, the brigands bit their lips and shuffled uneasily.

"This man's god really has given him great power," muttered one.

"Fancy being able to kill someone without touching him," marvelled another. "Scary, isn't it?"

"Yes. We shouldn't have tried to test him," said a third and there was a low murmur of agreement.

But Patrick and Mac Cuill were staring into each other's eyes as if there were no one else there.

"Why did you try to trap me?" Patrick asked, not unkindly because he sensed how desperately unhappy Mac Cuill really was.

Tears rose in the brigand's dark eyes.

"I'm so sorry," he choked. "I'll do whatever you tell me, if only you'll help me to get rid of this terrible feeling of guilt. I can't bear it any more."

Patrick went to him and laid a friendly hand on his arm.

"Believe in the true God," he urged. "Confess your wrongdoing and accept baptism in his name. Then all will be well, I promise you."

Mac Cuill looked like a drowning man who had been thrown a lifeline.

"Oh, I shall," he promised, but when he looked down at Earnán he gave a cry of pain and despair. "Only, what shall we do about this poor dead man?"

"Don't worry," replied Patrick calmly. "Earnán will rise up and live." All eyes were fixed on Patrick as he knelt and made the sign of the Cross over Earnán. Immediately the young man's mouth closed and his eyelids flickered. "Up you come," said Patrick, giving Earnán his hand.

By the time Earnán was on his feet, all the others

were on their knees.

That night Patrick, Beannán and Brógán had the novel experience of eating and sleeping in a bandit's cave. Mac Cuill insisted on entertaining them, and although Patrick had great difficulty in heaving himself up the cliff-face he knew the invitation couldn't be turned down. Long after his young companions had eaten their fill and fallen asleep on a pile of animal skins, Patrick and Mac Cuill sat at the mouth of the cave. Moonbeams explored the glen, making pale green patterns among the black rocks. Everything was hushed and very beautiful.

"My advice is to begin your new life somewhere else," Patrick said. "God has already forgiven you – he did that this afternoon when you told him you were sorry and let me baptise you. But you won't forgive yourself until you've done something to show your repentance, and you won't trust God totally until you've been alone with him in a dangerous situation."

This made sense to Mac Cuill.

"What do you suggest?" he asked anxiously.

"I think you should leave Ireland," Patrick said. "Give your stolen gold to the poor and take only the clothes you're wearing. When you reach the coast, find a coracle and put to sea – without an oar, if you have the courage. Give God the opportunity to look after you and take you where he wants you to go. I think you'll be glad later on."

"I'll do as you say," promised Mac Cuill.

In the morning Patrick, Beannán and Brógán said goodbye to Mac Cuill and his friends and continued their journey. Out in the open it was another perfect summer day. Invisible insects whirred in the grass and high clouds lightly dappled the hillside with shadow. A couple of miles beyond the glen they came upon Odhrán, lazing against the wheel of the cart while the pony munched the turf nearby.

"I came round the hill and got here last night," he said as he coaxed the reluctant animal between the shafts. "What kept you?"

Odhrán sounded more curious than worried. He had got used to Patrick's ways long ago.

"Business," Patrick airily replied.

Beannán and Brógán couldn't resist rolling their eyes and making faces behind his back. Odhrán grinned.

"I've caught some brown trout and picked blueberries for our dinner," was all he said.

In the heat of the afternoon, Brógán and Beannán dawdled far behind the cart. Patrick would have been cross if he had known that instead of praying they were talking over the events of the previous day, but again, they couldn't resist.

"Do you think Earnán was really dead?" Brógán asked, furrowing his dark brows.

Beannán shrugged his shoulders and shook his bright head.

"Maybe," he replied. "I don't suppose it matters very much. The miracle was really about something else, wasn't it?"

21

Writing Things Down

⚭

During the next winter Patrick stayed at Ard Mhacha.
He was grateful for a cell to shelter him from the wind
and sleet, and for the refreshing company of young
people. Otherwise it was a bad time for him. He
desperately missed Beannán, who had gone away to
study for the priesthood, and at the darkest time of
year some terrible news reached him. The soldiers of
Coroticus, a Scottish chieftain who claimed to be a
Christian, had raided the Irish coast and taken into
cruel slavery men and women whom Patrick had
himself baptised.

This news roused in Patrick half-forgotten memories
of his own abduction from Bannavem Taberniae more
than fifty years before. He remembered vividly the fear
and homesickness, the anxiety about family left behind.
In a fury he fired off a letter to Coroticus and his
soldiers, demanding the release of his converts. When it
was reported back to him that his words had been
received with jeering contempt he wrote again, a long,
pleading letter with an anguished cry to God at its heart.

"What am I to do, God? Lord, I am despised. See how your sheep are torn to pieces and carried off by pirates on the order of wicked Coroticus."

Patrick thought night and day of the white-robed, happy people he had anointed and baptised, and his grief for them was almost unbearable. Then, as January snow filled the ditch and drifted in peaks against the monastery fence, a messenger came toiling from the east with bad tidings of another kind.

Ever since Patrick had been sent to Ireland, against the wishes of some of the British clergy before whom his false friend Amicus had denounced him, he had known that he had enemies in Britain. Over the years he had heard of spiteful remarks and petty criticisms of the way he did his job. Patrick had ignored these because he was too busy to bother with them. But this time it seemed that a really slanderous accusation had been made.

"I'm sorry, Father," said the messenger, a young deacon whom Patrick knew well. "It disgusts me to mention such a falsehood but I have to warn you of what's being said. In Britain you're being accused of taking gifts of money and jewels from your converts and –" the young man gulped in embarrassment "– and keeping them for yourself."

Patrick could scarcely believe his ears. Since the day when he had given away the gold coins he had saved for Míleac he had been among the poorest men in Ireland. He felt his face going scarlet.

"I've never taken the smallest coin from anyone," he said thickly.

The messenger bowed his head.

"I know – but try telling them that," he replied miserably.

Patrick had every intention of telling them. His first thought was that he would go to Britain and defend himself, but when he'd had time to consider that didn't seem such a good idea. Not only had he vowed to spend the rest of his life in Ireland, but he couldn't bear to leave his people. His dealings with Coroticus had reminded him how easily a Christian convert could slip back into pagan ways. How could he be sure, if he spent the best part of a year away in Britain, that he wouldn't find backsliding in the Irish church on his return? Patrick was growing old and he knew perfectly well that he must die, but he had always trusted God to keep him alive until Beannán was ready to succeed him.

In the end, he sat down once more to write. In the flickering light of a tiny lamp he grasped a pen in his cold, gnarled fingers and dipped it in his inkpot.

"I, Patrick," he wrote, "am a sinner and a most unlearned man. I am the least of all the faithful, and I am greatly despised by many."

This was what he really thought about himself. His Latin was rusty and most of the learning he had struggled to acquire long ago at Autissiodorum had deserted him. What he did remember, with the clarity of old age, was his young life and God's goodness to him. As Patrick laboriously wrote down the story of his capture by pirates, his encounter with God beside the Wood of Foclath and his journey with the sailors and their dogs, all the sights and sounds of youth came flooding back to him. Sitting hunched in his cell with the wind gusting round his feet, the old man saw the snug villa at Bannavem Taberniae, heard the bleating of Míleac's lambs, smelt the salty tang of the sea.

Patrick knew that the story of his life was his best defence against the malicious lies of his enemies, but he couldn't help feeling angry and indignant that he should have to defend himself at all. At last he laid down his pen and gathered the closely written sheets into a bundle.

"Take it away," he said to Brógán, who for some time had acted as his secretary. "Make a copy to be kept here in Ireland and I'll send the original to Britain. Not that I suppose it will make any difference," he added bitterly. "They've always been unfair to me, and they aren't likely to change now."

The distress in Patrick's voice hurt Brógán, but he answered steadily.

"It isn't important what they think in Britain, Father. What matters is what we think here in Ireland. You're our bishop, after all."

22

The Birds

⊗

Now the seasons began to slip past Patrick in a sequence of white, spring green, emerald and gold. Like all old people he had the illusion that time passed more quickly than when he was young. No sooner, it seemed, had he admired the frilly spring leaves than a dabble of red in the hedges warned him of autumn's approach. Although he was tired and sore, a sense of urgency made Patrick restless. There was so much work still to do.

Always, between late February and October, he was on the road with Odhrán and an eager group of younger friends. He still loved the preaching and the singing and the fellowship of the camp, but sometimes he couldn't help remembering nostalgically the distant days when he was alone with God in deserted places. As he aged, the longing grew in him to find somewhere high and lonely where he might recapture that experience one more time.

On a February morning, when the streams were chuckling and a pale sun was drawing up steam from the wet thatch, Patrick called Odhrán to walk with him in the oakwood near Dáire's farm.

"I need to exercise my legs," he said, "and there's something I want to discuss with you." Odhrán's lips twitched in his greying beard. He knew what Patrick meant by "discussion" – the unfolding of a plan which he had worked out last night in bed. But he didn't comment as he followed the old man under the mossy branches, picking his way among the silver streams that veined the squelchy forest floor. Patrick came suddenly to the point. "Listen," he said. "How long do you suppose it would take us to get to Cruachán Acla?"

This wasn't what Odhrán had been expecting.

"Cruachán Acla?" he repeated, visualising the lonely, cone-shaped mountain he had seen from a distance on earlier journeys in to the west. "Why on earth do you want to go to Cruachán Acla? Not much work to be done there, unless you fancy preaching to the birds."

Patrick allowed this kind of cheek from Odhrán in private. They had been friends for a very long time.

"Just answer the question," he said mildly.

Odhrán wrinkled his forehead as he did some working-out in his head.

"If we went straight there," he said eventually, "it would take about four weeks. With our normal stops and detours, twice as long."

"Good," said Patrick in satisfaction. "We'll be going straight there." His next words took Odhrán's breath away. "I've decided to spend the forty days of Lent on the summit of the mountain. I need some time alone with God."

Odhrán gasped. He looked at Patrick with wide, incredulous eyes.

"You can't be serious," he said vehemently. "It's the most desolate place I've ever seen. Do you really want to die among the rocks and have your bones picked clean by scavenging birds?"

Patrick shrugged his shoulders.

"I don't care what happens to my bones," he said, "after my spirit leaves them." Then he gave Odhrán a determined grey look and added firmly, "You and Brógán can come with me to the mountain's foot. I want you all packed up and ready to leave at dawn tomorrow."

So much for discussion, thought Odhrán ruefully as he followed the limping figure out of the wood.

Afterwards, when it was all over, Patrick would marvel at the strength God had given him for what proved to be the most trying experience of his long life. At the time, his one thought was that having started, he must see it through. After a long, fatiguing journey he came with Odhrán and Brógán to the foot of Cruachán Acla, close to the western sea.

"Won't you take some food, Father?" Odhrán begged, offering a bag containing barley cake and some lumps of cheese.

"Let me come with you as far as the summit," suggested Brógán. "I'm strong. You can lean on me."

It hurt Patrick to ignore their affectionate pleas, but he felt he had no choice.

"Our Lord endured forty days and nights alone in the wilderness," he reminded them. "For his sake, I shall do the same. God will protect me, as he protected him."

Patrick spoke confidently. Yet as he prepared to leave his companions he had a premonition that his days on the mountain-top would not be the godly, peaceful time he had imagined. Like Christ in the wilderness, he would be tested to breaking-point. Patrick shivered, but he wasn't tempted for more than an instant to change his mind. Taking nothing but an ash-plant stick and a small iron bell which his friend Bríd had given him, he said goodbye and went on his way.

It was a long, painful climb. Heaving up his frail old body on his stick, slipping on loose gravel and grazing his poorly shod feet, Patrick struggled upward through a storm of March wind and rain. The summit of the mountain was bald and cheerless, and as he wrapped himself in his cloak and lay down in the lee of a rock, he didn't feel at all like the strong lad who had sat on the hillside minding Míleac's sheep. Patrick tried to comfort himself with the words of a psalm: *He shall cover thee with his feathers, and under his wings shalt thou trust* . . . Yet he couldn't help wondering bleakly whether Odhrán had been right. His bones might indeed be picked by birds of prey in this desolate place.

Even so, the first few days were tolerable enough. On the second morning the wind dropped and the clouds receded. Walking for exercise between stints of prayer, Patrick appreciated the view. To the east he looked out over a land of brown peat bogs and silver lakes. To the west he saw the grey ocean rolling and heaving itself over the rim of the world. When night fell he huddled in the little stone shelter he had made for himself, praising God for the wonder of the moon and stars.

Patrick was used to hardship and cold, and ate so sparsely that at the beginning of his vigil lack of food scarcely affected him. Only gradually did hunger begin to gnaw first at his body, then at his mind.

Patrick had always liked birds, but on top of Cruachán Acla they were a nuisance. Grey gulls and gannets, landing in a loud disturbance of wings, interrupted his prayers with their harsh cries. For a while he managed to scare them off by ringing his bell and flapping his cloak, but they soon got used to that. Then one day, when he was becoming too weak and light-headed even to crawl out of his shelter, Patrick became aware of something sinister. The gulls and gannets seemed to have changed into ravens. At first he told himself not to be absurd, but every time he raised his eyelids he saw them again. Black and predatory, they clung to the rocks with hideous, hooky feet and watched Patrick with cold, reptilian eyes.

God help me, Patrick thought in terror. These birds are demons and it isn't only my body they want to devour. They want my soul too. Only iron determination prevented him from clawing his way across the summit and slithering down the mountain. For days he crouched in his shelter with his hands over his face, praying for God's protection against the power of evil. But as he grew weaker and hunger tore at his belly like a sharp-toothed rat, God had never seemed so far away. Patrick lost count of the days and nights as the birds became the outer form of thoughts almost too terrible to bear.

Every doubt, every anxiety he had ever felt and suppressed came back to torment him. Was his life worth anything at all, he wondered. Had God really forgiven the sin of his boyhood which no one in Ireland knew about? Had he been right to leave his parents to an unknown and perhaps terrible fate? Had he been responsible for the deaths of Míleac and the druid Lochra? All the good he had done seemed trivial to Patrick now. Darkness enveloped him and he came close to doubting the existence of God.

But not quite. At long last, when his head throbbed and the sky was frantic with beating wings, Patrick somehow gathered the tatters of his strength. Clutching his bell he dragged himself to his feet and tottered out among the rocks.

"Hear me, demons!" he cried, making the sign of the Cross. "I order you to leave me, in the name of the Father, the Son and the Holy Spirit!"

Gritting his teeth, Patrick swung his bell and threw it as hard as he could among the birds. For a moment it seemed as if both bell and birds were frozen in mid air. Then the bell came down, clanging as its side split against a rock. With a great, desolate cry the birds wheeled overhead and flew straight out to sea. As Patrick fell on his knees they shrank into a small black cloud which finally vaporised on the evening sky.

Patrick went on kneeling on the mountain-top long after the birds had gone. All the dark thoughts had departed from his mind and he felt himself wrapped in a cloak of peace. For a moment he saw a ring of white doves hovering above his head and heard a chiming, angelic voice.

"The eternal God is thy refuge, and underneath are the everlasting arms."

23

Beyond Díchú's Barn

❧

Odhrán and Brógán would never forget the joy they felt on an April morning when they saw Patrick's familiar figure staggering down the mountain side. Eagerly they ran to greet him and help him down the last stony stretch to their camp. But if they had imagined that Patrick would now rest quietly for a week or two before allowing himself to be driven back to Ard Mhacha, they were mistaken. No sooner had Patrick eaten some bread and cheese than he was making plans again.

"I suppose I'd better rest for a couple of days," he said in the tone of someone irked by his own weakness. "But no longer, mind. We're going to work our way down the coast as far as the Shannon. If we go north-west from there, we should get to Díchú's barn by August. I'd like to be back at Ard Mhacha in time for the fruit harvest."

Odhrán opened his mouth to protest but there was no point. Patrick had crawled on to a pile of sheepskins under the cart and was already fast asleep.

In one way, Patrick made a quick recovery from his ordeal on Cruachán Acla. Happy in the certainty of God's love and forgiveness, he enjoyed a summer spent visiting old friends and making new converts in lonely villages and farms. Yet in another way he was never the same again. Slowly his restlessness and anxiety about his unfinished work left him, and he accepted that the future was for God to decide. He still cared for his companions, but a feeling of detachment from worldly things grew in him until he seemed to see even them at a distance. They were like people who would always be dear to him, but who now lived far away. Patrick knew that this was his last long journey. He would never again see the ocean and he was looking at the lakes and fells of Connacht for the last time.

Death, however, was still some way off. That September there was a great reunion of friends at Díchú's place, now known simply as "Sabhall", the Barn. To Patrick's great joy Beannán joined him with the news that he was to complete his studies at Ard Mhacha. Good news also awaited Patrick in a letter from Bishop Conindrus, who lived on the island of Monavia between Ireland and Britain. Mac Cuill mac Greacha, having taken Patrick's advice, had been cast up in an oarless coracle on the Monavian shore. Conindrus and his assistant Rumilus had found him and taken him into their household.

"Conindrus says that Mac Cuill is determined to lead a good, holy life," Patrick told Beannán with satisfaction. "He thinks Mac Cuill even hopes to become a priest one day."

Beannán thought of the ugly brigand who had

scared him and Brógán stiff in the mountain pass. He laughed and shook his fair head.

"Perhaps Mac Cuill will become a bishop," he said.

He spoke half in jest, but Patrick replied seriously.

"Certainly he will," he said. "And certainly so will you."

As he had wished, Patrick was back in Ard Mhacha in time to see the apples stored in the barn with the winnowed barley. As the leaves fell he settled to a quiet existence of reading and prayer. Sometimes he felt he wasn't really living any more, only waiting patiently for Beannán to finish his studies and release him. It was about this time that he began to have visions of an angel whom he had glimpsed at intervals throughout his life. The angel's name was Victor, and he spoke reassuringly of the heavenly kingdom.

To Victor Patrick voiced his deepest longings for the church and people of Ireland. He prayed that there would always be a Christian bishop in his city of Ard Mhacha and he had a special, personal request that God would show mercy to the descendants of Díchú, his first convert. He hoped that everyone who died with a hymn of his on his lips would be blessed and one day, when he was feeling bolder than usual, he begged to be allowed to judge his dear Irish on the Last Day. Patrick was rather disappointed when Victor didn't respond immediately to these prayers.

None of his friends really expected the old man to leave Ard Mhacha again, but Patrick never ceased to surprise them. Whenever the sun strengthened and leaves thickened on willow and birch, a lifetime's habitual wanderlust quickened the frail old bones. For

several summers Patrick moved in easy stages from Ard
Mhacha to Sabhall, staying with friends along the
route. He loved the weeks spent in Díchú's house and
was secretly proud that he could still preach to the
crowds flocking to the first church he had founded. He
always returned to his cell at Ard Mhacha, however,
before winter set in, and when one year he fell ill and
was unable to leave Sabhall at the usual time he found
it hard not to fret.

"We'll have to wait until spring, Father," said
Brógán one late October morning, as he stood at the
door watching drifts of cold grey drizzle blowing from
the eastern sea. "You can't possibly travel in weather
like this."

Brógán did his best to speak calmly and conceal the
anguish he felt. In his heart, he believed that Patrick
would be dead by the year's end. Díchú and Odhrán
were convinced that the fragile old body couldn't
withstand another attack of fever and chest pain, and
although he wanted to scream that they were wrong,
Brógán had to agree. Yet Patrick lingered beyond
Christmas, often dragging himself from his bed to a
seat by the fire and even tottering as far as the church
when there was a lull in the wet, stormy weather. He
too knew that he was dying, but he was secretly
determined to die at Ard Mhacha. On a February
morning when thin sunlight was spilling through the
open door of Díchú's kitchen, he summoned Odhrán.

"Get the cart ready," he said abruptly. "We're going
home." And before Odhrán could roar a refusal he
added firmly, "I'm still your bishop, Odhrán. I will be
obeyed."

Odhrán knew he had no choice. With a heavy heart he went to call Brógán, Beannán and the other friends from Ard Mhacha who had gathered anxiously at Sabhall. In worried silence they harnessed a pony and made a bed of sheepskins and woollen blankets for Patrick in the back of the cart. Patrick embraced Díchú and his family and said goodbye.

The sky was the colour of a duck's egg and the air was mild. Revived by delight because he was actually on the road home, Patrick sat up in the back of the cart, enjoying the sunshine and the gurgling of water released at last from the stranglehold of ice. The colours of the countryside, brown, coral and straw, were gentle on Patrick's tired eyes. So when he saw, up ahead by the roadside, a bush glowing with fiery red leaves, the contrast startled him. As the cart trundled closer, he realised two things. The bush really was on fire, and he was the only one who knew it.

"Stop, Odhrán!" Patrick cried, and Odhrán at once drew the cart to a halt.

"Is something wrong, Father?" he asked, and Patrick's other companions clustered anxiously round.

Their concern deepened when they saw Patrick on his knees, staring rapturously at what seemed to them an ordinary thorn bush, still bearing some of last year's ragged leaves. But Patrick saw a wonderful, burning bush like the one that had appeared to Moses on Mount Sinai long ago. The angel Victor stood unflinching in the flames.

"Listen, Patrick," Victor said. "It is not God's will that you should die at Ard Mhacha. You must go back to Sabhall. If you do, God will grant the requests you

123

made about the future of your church and people."

Victor then gave some instructions which surprised Patrick, but he promised to obey.

"Odhrán, turn the cart," he said as the angel vanished and the blazing bush became an unremarkable wayside shrub. "We're going back to Sabhall."

"Whatever you say, Father," agreed Odhrán, shaking the pony's reins.

Díchú was more relieved than amazed when Patrick and his friends arrived back in the yard barely seven hours after their departure. He and his wife had been convinced that a sick old man couldn't endure a journey of seventy miles over rough countryside and had feared that he would die on the road. At Patrick's request Beannán and Brógán made up a bed in the church, close to the altar. All of Patrick's friends took turns at looking after him, but it was to his adopted son Beannán that he whispered his final orders.

"When I'm dead," he said, "you mustn't bury my body here or take it back to Ard Mhacha. The angel Victor has given me instructions, and since you are my heir, you must see that they are obeyed. Do you promise?"

"Of course, Father," replied Beannán hoarsely.

His throat was tight with grief and the light of the sanctuary lamp was blurred by his unshed tears.

"Listen, then," said Patrick, clasping Beannán's hand kindly in his. "Once I'm dead you must lay my body on a wagon and put two oxen between the shafts. Don't try to guide them, but let them pull the wagon wherever they choose. Where they finally stop will be the right place for my burial."

Patrick didn't speak much after that. Drifting in and out of consciousness, he dreamed of the Cumbrian hills of his childhood and the night sky above the Wood of Foclath. He breathed in the scent of sweet, wet grass and heard again the voices of the sea. In the middle of March, having received the Sacrament, he died.

Afterwards strange stories were told of that time. It was said that on the night following Patrick's death angels kept watch over his body, leaving behind them the fragrance of honey and wine. It was also reported that on that night no darkness fell: "It did not wrap its black wings around the earth, and the evening did not send the darkness which carries the stars."

No one is really sure where Patrick's bones finally rested, but there is a long tradition that the oxen drawing the funeral wagon stopped two miles from Sabhall at Dún Leathghlaise. There is also a legend that, years later, two other great saints of Ireland were buried there too. In the twelfth century Bishop Malachy of Down saw in a vision lines carved on stone:

In Down, three saints one grave do fill:
Patrick, Bríd and Colm Cille.